ALBERT

CAMUS

ALBERT CAMUS

ELEMENTS OF A LIFE

ROBERT ZARETSKY

CORNELL UNIVERSITY PRESS

ITHACA AND LONDON

First published 2010 by Cornell University Press
Printed in the United States of America

Book design by Scott Levine

Library of Congress Cataloging-in-Publication Data

Zaretsky, Robert, 1955–
    Albert Camus, elements of a life / Robert Zaretsky.
      p. cm.
    Includes bibliographical references and index.
    ISBN 978-0-8014-4805-8 (cloth : alk. paper)
  1. Camus, Albert, 1913–1960—Criticism and interpretation.   I. Title.

    PQ2605.A3734Z97   2010
    848'.91409—dc22

                                                2009034850

Cornell University Press strives to use environmentally responsible sup-
pliers and materials to the fullest extent possible in the publishing of
its books. Such materials include vegetable-based, low-VOC inks and
acid-free papers that are recycled, totally chlorine-free, or partly composed
of nonwood fibers. For further information, visit our website at www.
cornellpress.cornell.edu.

Cloth printing   10 9 8 7 6 5 4 3 2 1

Frontispiece—Kurt Hutton/Hulton Archive/Getty Images

FOR TED ESTESS

CONTENTS

ACKNOWLEDGMENTS

This small book is the work of many people. At the University of Houston, the provost, John Antel, and the dean emeritus of the Honors College, Ted Estess, conspired to provide me with a semester's leave that allowed me to meet my deadline. William Monroe, dean of the Honors College, and Joseph Pratt, dean of the College of Liberal Arts and Social Sciences, also offered critical support. Colleagues at Houston—Sarah Fishman, Ted Estess, and Dorothy Baker—read and commented on parts of the manuscript, as did my friend John Scott. My French publisher, David Gaussen, has been an enthusiastic and sharp-eyed reader. Jeffrey Isaac spoke up for the book when it was still just an idea, while David Carroll saved me from making a number of historical and textual errors. My copyeditor Jane Todd did a superb job, as did Cornell's editorial team, led by Susan Specter and Susan Barnett. Peter Potter has, as always, gracefully balanced the demands of friendship and criticism. This is no less true of my wife, Julie Zaretsky: she knows how much I owe her. Finally, I am indebted to Tzvetan Todorov, Alice Conklin, and David Mikics. Despite their own busy lives, they read and re-read the entire work, sharing their excitement and hesitations, encouragement and doubts, insights and corrections. They made this a far better book than it otherwise would have been, and I alone am responsible for the remaining weaknesses.

For more than twenty years, my friend and mentor Ted Estess has shown those around him what it means to attend to the world and to others. I dedicate this book to him.

ALBERT

CAMUS

REGARDING CAMUS

"We live with a few familiar ideas. Two or three," Albert Camus once wrote. "We polish and transform them according to the societies and the men we happen to meet. It takes ten years to have an idea that is really one's own—that one can talk about."[1] By the same token, the world has long had a few familiar ideas about the author of *The Stranger* and *The Plague*, *The Myth of Sisyphus*, and *The Rebel*. There is the idea of a Camus who probed the notions of freedom and justice, who reflected on the dangers of either notion becoming an absolute claim, and who tried to reconcile their conflicting characters. There is also the idea of a Camus who wrote about the nature of exile both from one's native land—in his case, French Algeria—and from a world bereft of a god. And there is the idea of a Camus who gave voice to an entire spectrum of silence: the silence of childhood innocence, the silence of the political prisoner or disenfranchised native, the silence of tragic conflicts, and the silence of a cosmos indifferent to our need for meaning.

These ideas about Camus not only constitute elements of his life but also explain the abiding relevance his work has for our lives. Like many others of my generation, I first read Camus in high school. I carried him in my backpack while traveling across Europe, I carried him into (and out of) relationships, and I carried him into (and out of) difficult periods of my life. More recently, I have carried him into university classes that I have taught, coming out of them with a renewed appreciation for his art. To be sure, my idea of Camus thirty years ago scarcely resembles my idea of him today. While my admiration and attachment to his writings remain as great as they were long ago, the reasons are now more complicated and critical.

One constant in my understanding of Camus's significance over these many years is how, until his untimely death in 1960, he wrestled with certain ideas and shared this struggle with readers. The quality of that struggle—engaged in with an intellectual integrity that led to a fortifying hopelessness—has marked all who have read him. If there is one conviction that scholars and nonscholars share, it is that Camus is still an indispensable companion in our intellectual and ethical lives. He appears to us, in a way that few other writers do, as someone who wrote for his life and for our lives as well.

This book is neither a full biography nor a scholarly commentary. It is an essay in which I trace the ways these "familiar ideas" weave through Camus's life. Each chapter is devoted to a specific event: Camus's visit to Kabylia in 1939 to report on the conditions of the local Berber tribes; his decision to sign a petition to commute the collaborationist writer Robert Brasillach's death sentence in 1945; his famous quarrel with his friend Jean-Paul Sartre in 1952 over the nature of communism; his silence over the war in Algeria after 1956. Given the importance of each of these moments, I take the liberty of moving back and forth across time and space in order to explore the many layers of its significance. Moreover, I deliberately bring to the fore individuals and ideas that other accounts often leave in the background. The reader will find discussions of the Greek writers Thucydides and Aeschylus, the religious thinkers Augustine and Rousseau, the French essayists Michel de Montaigne and Sébastien-Roch Nicolas Chamfort, and even the Irish nationalist playwright J. M. Synge. Some of them, like Synge and Chamfort, gave Camus unexpected ways to express his own concerns; others, like the ancient Greeks, exerted a greater influence than is usually recognized. These thinkers are not walk-ons in the story of Camus's life; instead, Camus turns to them during the most critical moments.

One other thinker, though not discussed in the book, is nevertheless present: Simone Weil. After World War II, Camus, under the auspices of the publishing house Gallimard, founded a series called "Espoir" (Hope). He published Weil's L'enracinement, subsequently translated into English as The Need for Roots, in this series. A recurrent concern in Weil's thought is what she called the work of attention. This elusive yet crucial human activity is not simply "paying attention," drawing an object closer to us and placing it under a magnifying glass. It is not even necessarily seeing with one's own eyes. Instead, it is stepping back and waiting for the object to draw closer to you. It is apprehending the world and others, as free as possible from the psychological scrims our egos are forever building. Weil compared the attentive individual to a "man on a mountain who, as he looks forward, sees also below him, without actually looking at them, a great many forests and plains."[2] While her (unorthodox) Christian faith, along with her transcendental grounding of the work of attention, separated her from Camus, in her description of the activity itself she closely mirrors Camus's sensibility. One of the great constants in Camus's work and life is precisely this kind of attentiveness. It is a quality that marks not just his fictional characters but often their creator as well.

When we attend to others, we tend to listen rather than talk. For this reason, the other side to the coin of attentiveness is silence. Camus's artistry and morality are, in part, expressed by such silences. There are the silences that shimmer like mirages in the austere Algerian landscapes, and those in which so many of his characters are steeped as they regard the world. There is also the silence in which Camus wrapped himself in the late 1950s as French Algeria collapsed into war. Born in Algeria and raised with the values of republican France, Camus was torn between the competing and ultimately irreconcilable claims represented by French imperialism and Algerian nationalism. Finally, in 1957, he declared he would no longer speak about the war in public—a vow that, with two exceptions, he kept until his death three years later.

Much noise has inevitably swirled around this silence ever since. So, too, for a different kind of silence that hovered over Camus during his last years. By the early 1950s, Camus felt stifled and emptied; he feared he had fallen silent because he no longer had anything to say as an artist. The violent public quarrel with Sartre over Camus's philosophical essay *The Rebel* led not just to the end of their friendship but also to deepening doubts on Camus's part about his art. As he told one friend, "I feel like ink absorbed by a wad of paper."[3] The subsequent publication of his novel *The Fall* lifted these doubts, but only for a time. When Camus received the Nobel Prize for Literature in 1957, some critics thought he was too young for the award (he had just turned forty-four). For others, however, Camus was too old and washed up: the prize, they concluded, confirmed that Camus was a literary relic who had nothing more to say. Camus shared these doubts: in his short story "Jonas, or the Artist at Work," he portrays an artist whose life slowly empties of creativity, an artist reduced to staring at a blank canvas.

Though first written several years before, the story was published in his 1957 collection of short stories, *Exile and the Kingdom,* and spoke clearly to Camus's predicament.

Camus's emphasis on silence, in his art and in his politics, mirrored his determination to speak for others who, in various ways, were condemned to silence. In his Nobel address, Camus declared that art's nobility is rooted in "the refusal to lie about what one knows, and the resistance to oppression."[4] Camus described and denounced the plight of French Algeria's Arab and Berber populations at a time when these peoples were all but invisible to most French citizens. Immediately after the war, he no less forcefully decried France's use of torture in Algeria, horrified by the ways in which the French, so recently oppressed under the Germans, had become the Arabs' oppressor. Then there was his stubborn battle against French government censors during the early months of World War II, when he tirelessly combated the "sophistic claim that a nation's morale entails the sacrifice of its freedoms."[5] This claim, along with his condemnation of the French republic's outlawing of the Communist Party after the declaration of war—"law concerns us all" and cannot be applied selectively—apply not just to other crises in Camus's time but also to those we confront in our own.[6] The urgency of Camus's voice still claims our attention, and his lucidity still serves as a model.

Many critics have rightly observed that Camus's stubborn humanism looms especially large today. If we are not careful, however, we will miss just how extraordinary his stance was and remains. This does not mean he was a saint—on the contrary, Camus's colleagues, friends, and family offer ample witness to his flaws. Looking back on his quarrel with Sartre, we are torn between horror at Sartre's attack of his former friend in the pages of *Les Temps Modernes* and unease over the intellectual and personal shortcomings in Camus that Sartre rightly identified. Paradoxically, some of

Camus's virtues also blur his significance. His battle against totalitarianism, courageous in his own day, has since become orthodoxy. His loathing of the Algerian nationalist movement, the Front de Libération Nationale (FLN), has been largely justified by the subsequent history of an Algeria ruled by a single party. His efforts to lay a foundation for morality, viewed as quaint by many of his contemporaries, have since been joined by many thinkers. And who today would dispute his passionate defense of the necessity for direct and sincere dialogue? In a way, the world—or, at least, those who devote their lives to analyzing it—has caught up to Camus.

The problem, however, is that most of us are quite comfortable with these positions: our morality and our humanism seem easily learned but scarcely earned. I doubt that Camus, were he alive today, would feel at home in the company of either the neoliberal or the neoconservative thinkers who claim him as an inspiration. Instead, he would still be an exile and an outsider—a moralist who, as Tony Judt remarks, is by nature uneasy with himself and his world.[7] In part, this stems from Camus's insight into the fundamental nature of life. His work touches on the mystery—for better or worse, he called it the "absurdity"—of the human condition and its resistance to meaning. It is the human being's confrontation with the universe, not something inherent to the universe itself, that leads to absurdity. "The absurd," Camus wrote in *The Myth of Sisyphus*, "depends as much on man as on the world."[8] At such moments, wading in a sea we thought we knew, we are suddenly knocked off our feet by a kind of metaphysical riptide.

Camus insisted that absurdity does not lead to a nihilistic life. On the contrary, the very ability to acknowledge the absurd requires a moral effort. "All I can hope to do," he said shortly after World War II, "is show that generous forms of behavior can be engendered even in a world without God and that man alone in the universe can still create his own values. That is, in my opinion, the sole problem posed by our era."[9]

And it remains one of the great problems of our era. Camus's writings have become guides for the perplexed—a status that left Camus uncomfortable. "I speak for no one," he insisted. "I have enough difficulty speaking for myself. I don't know, or I know only dimly, where I am headed." While an element of false modesty was at play, there was also a deep element of sincerity. Camus became the voice of a generation with dizzying speed: he published his first novel, *The Stranger*, in 1942 and emerged from the war as the spokesperson for the Resistance and existentialism. Little more than a decade later, in 1957, he won the Nobel Prize. Then, on January 4, 1960, he was killed when a car in which he was riding in southern France swerved off the road and slammed into a tree.

o o o

When Camus died, he was carrying a briefcase that contained a handwritten text of nearly 150 pages. It was the manuscript of *Le premier homme* (*The First Man*), a novel he had begun writing in earnest after winning the Nobel Prize. Early in the unfinished novel, the hero, Jacques Cormery—like Camus, a middle-aged French Algerian—visits a military cemetery in the Breton town of Saint-Brieuc. Guided by the caretaker, Cormery finds the reason for his visit: a simple gravestone with the inscription "Henri Cormery, 1885–1914." Jacques Cormery was scarcely a year old when his father was killed in the Battle of the Marne. As he gazes at the stone, Cormery "automatically did the arithmetic: twenty-nine years. Suddenly he was struck by an idea that shook his very being. He was forty years old. The man buried under that slab, who had been his father, was younger than he."[10]

At this point, both Cormery and Camus begin the search for their pasts. But while *The First Man* is Camus's most personal work, it is not unique in that respect. Throughout his short life as a writer, Camus implicated himself in his art: behind his sharp and chiseled phrases throb powerful memories, experiences, concerns, and passions. One of his close friends, Jean de Maisonseul, found that Camus used the first-person *je* too often in his first collection of essays, *L'Envers et l'endroit*—a gentle accusation that Camus accepted: a writer "needs to remain behind the scenes," he admitted.[11] In a preface he wrote to a new edition of the essays in 1958, Camus insists on their personal nature: "This little book has considerable value as testimony."[12] And this is no less true of his last work, *The First Man*, which Camus used the way others use memoir, as an effort to cast his past into meaningful shape.

Camus once confessed he "never recovered" from his harsh and spare childhood.[13] Camus's family resided in the Belcourt neighborhood of Algiers in an apartment with three small rooms and a kitchen, no plumbing, no electricity, and just one toilet shared by the three families in the building. He lived there from infancy until high school with his grandmother, mother, brother, and uncle; as for Camus's father, Lucien Camus, he, like Henri Cormery, had died in the Battle of the Marne in 1914. All that his widow retained was a photograph and a fragment of the shell that had killed him. Camus and his older brother, Lucien, shared a single bed, wedged into the same room with their mother's bed; the sole window gave onto the inner courtyard. The grandmother had a room to herself, while her brother, Camus's Uncle Etienne, slept in a room that also served as the dining area. Under the dull yellow glow of a hanging oil lamp was a single table where the family ate, the children did their homework, and Etienne cleaned his hunting gun and picked the fleas from his dog, Brillant, all under the grandmother's fierce glare.

In an early essay, Camus reveals the impact his childhood home had on his life. The story's narrator sits in an otherwise empty Arab café in Algiers as night falls, deep in thought about the "child who lived in a poor neighborhood." He recalls his old house so well that he could go back there on the darkest night and climb the unlit stairs "without stumbling once.... His legs retain the exact height of the steps; his hand, the instinctive, never-conquered horror of the banister. Because of the cockroaches."[14] The vermin came with the territory, as did the shadows and smells.

But the territory was veined with other and better memories as well. Belcourt was to interwar Algiers what the Lower East Side was to New York City in the interwar years: a densely populated neighborhood of poor but not destitute workers and artisans, professionals and shopkeepers, attracted to the host country by its credo of equality and opportunity. Most of the residents of Belcourt were European immigrants known as *pieds noirs:* Spaniards, Italians, Maltese, and a sizable Jewish community. The broad boulevards such as rue de Lyon were lined with ficus trees and laced with trolley lines, while the narrow streets were thick with small shops, workshops, and tenements, with knots of children playing *canette vinga* (a cross between tennis and stickball), all the while dodging pedestrians, street vendors, stray dogs, and squawking chickens.

The sea offered Camus and his friends what the Hudson River offered the youth of New York: an escape from the pounding summer heat of the city. During his postwar visit to New York, an uneasy Camus watched the traffic on Riverside Drive and thought of the sea: "The uninterrupted line of cars...sang dull and distant—exactly the sound of the waves."[15] It is a rare work by Camus that is not instilled with the author's abiding love of the Mediterranean. His literary characters, from Meursault in *The Stranger* to Rieux in *The Plague* or Cormery in *The First Man,* all find in the sea reprieve from the sound and fury of society. So, too, does Camus: only when he swims in the waters, then drops to the sand on the beaches of the Mediterranean does he become at one with the world. Under this sun, he "dons no mask."[16] The Mediterranean is a philosophical no less than a physical state, elevated by Camus to the symbol of an ancient world of human values and thought, profane, clasping the earth, a world he erected against the overreaching and dry ideologies he associated with the gray landscapes of urban Europe.

Yet there was one ideology whose importance Camus gladly credited: French republicanism. Until the end of his life, Camus remained attached to both the reality and the promise of France's republican credo. Upon the death of his father, Camus became a *pupille de la nation:* a ward of a state indebted to those who had been sacrificed on its behalf. Ever since 1870, the French secondary school system had taught its students not just how to read and write but how to be Frenchmen and -women. One of the republican school's fundamental tasks was the making of good citizens: men and women imbued with the progressive and egalitarian, rational and secular values bequeathed by the French Revolution.

The vanguard of this massive effort at civil pedagogy—in a sense, the missionaries of this new secular religion—were the primary school teachers. Known as *instituteurs,* they fanned out to the provinces, including Algeria, to carry the gospel of the republic. Few men better exemplified this mission than Louis Germain, who taught the ten-year-old Camus. A veteran of World War I, Germain took notice of the boy not only because he was a *pupille de la nation* but also because Camus's intelligence and intensity set him apart from his classmates. Germain persuaded Camus's grandmother and mother to allow him to take an examination that would provide an academic scholarship for the *lycée,* or high school. Though they were dubious—the grandmother, in particular, thought it better to have the boy apprenticed and earning a salary instead of idling away his time in a classroom—the family was swayed by Germain's eloquence. For several weeks, Germain tutored Camus and a couple of classmates every day after school. For the first time in their lives, the children felt "they existed and that they were the objects of the highest regard: they were judged worthy to discover the world."[17] Camus passed the exam and, he insisted, his life was changed forever.

Camus in fact discovered two worlds: one of material poverty, which clung to the spare and tattered family possessions in Belcourt, the other of spiritual wealth, found in the waves breaking in the distance and star-strewn sky sweeping over his head. His work and life were filled with the tension he felt between the kingdoms of scarcity and fullness, of society and nature; he had a palpable sense that he himself straddled the two realms. At night, the young Camus would gaze out the apartment window that gave onto the street: though overwhelmed by the smell of the "stinking corridor" behind him and the feel of the rotten seat bottom fraying under him, at the same time, "with eyes raised, he drank in the pure night."[18]

For Camus, the most overpowering memory of childhood was of silence. The grandmother, Catherine Sintes, a widow, bitter and violent, was unlettered and laconic; with Camus and his brother, Lucien, she often expressed herself with slaps and whippings rather than words. Uncle Etienne had been mute until his early teens; after an operation, he was able to speak, but only haltingly and simply, communicating "as much by onomatopoeic sounds and gestures as with the hundred-odd words at his disposal."[19] And his mother, also named Catherine, was illiterate and partly deaf. According to a family tradition, Catherine Sintes had been perfectly at ease speaking as a young woman; it was only in 1914, after she received news of the death of her husband, that her speech was hobbled.

It was when she lost her husband and her tongue that Catherine Camus lost what little freedom she had had. With the infant Albert and the toddler Lucien, she moved back in with her mother in Belcourt. She spent the rest of her life working long hours as a cleaning woman, returning to a home ruled by a harsh matriarch and to two sons whom she loved but was scarcely able to protect, much less nurture. When the grandmother grabbed her whip and began to beat one of the children, Catherine Sintes stood to one side, pleading only that she not strike him on the head. She was there, yet as elusive as the father Camus never knew; she was indispensable, but silent like the world that refused to surrender meaning; she filled her son's life, though the nature of her presence was forever an enigma.

When we are stripped down to a certain point, Camus wrote, "hope and despair are equally groundless and the whole of life can be summed up in an image."[20] For Camus, that image almost certainly was his mother. Even more than the sea, the figure of the silent mother occupies the center of Camus's writings; it is the sun, or perhaps the dark matter, toward which everything else is pulled. It is the death of Meursault's mother that begins the unmaking of his life; it is the mostly wordless presence of Rieux's mother that prevents the unmaking of a world swept by plague; it is under the silent gaze of his mother that Cormery begins the search for his past. As he began to piece together *The First Man* in the last years of his life, Camus wrote that the novel would repeat "the entire journey in order to discover his secret: he is not the first. Every man is the first man, nobody is. This is why he throws himself at his mother's feet."[21]

While this act does not lead to a final answer, it does lead to a deeper awareness of life's inexhaustible richness. When the young Camus would return to the apartment, he sometimes found his mother already there, "huddled in a chair, gazing in front of her, wandering off in the dizzy pursuit of a crack along the floor. As the night thickened around her, her muteness would seem irredeemably desolate." Camus would stand at the door, looking at "her thin shape and bony shoulders, and stop, afraid." Camus writes:

> He is beginning to feel a lot of things. He is scarcely aware of his own existence, but this animal silence makes him want to cry with

pain. He feels sorry for his mother; is this the same thing as loving her? She has never hugged or kissed him, for she wouldn't know how. He stands a long time watching her. Feeling separate from her, he becomes conscious of her suffering. She does not hear him, for she is deaf....The silence marks a pause, an immensely long moment. Vaguely aware of this, the child thinks the surge of feeling in him is love for his mother. And it must be, because after all she is his mother.[22]

The silence of shadows is a brute fact of life: it remains when everything else dies away; it is all that was before anything else comes into being. When Camus imagines his own birth in *The First Man*, he portrays his mother and father lying next to each other on mattresses that had been placed near a fireplace. The newborn "slept in silence except for an occasional weak gurgle," while an exhausted mother and father lay under a roof that had moments earlier rattled from a violent rainstorm. Silence also engulfs the room where Camus, now an adult, tends to his mother after she fainted in her apartment. Just as his own father did forty years before with his mother, now the son stretches himself out alongside her on the narrow bed; the silence that drapes itself over them is not unwelcome: "All that remained was a great garden of silence interrupted now and then by the sick woman's frightened moans....The world had melted away....Finally he fell asleep, but not without taking with him the tender and despairing image of two people's loneliness together."[23]

There are also the silences of sunlight—the calm of siesta time in Algiers, when the calls of Arab vendors underscore the lush sluggishness of time and the hush of the empty streets. But there is also the hammering silence that overwhelms Meursault on the beach in Algiers moments before he kills the Arab in *The Stranger*, the stillness of plague-ridden Oran in *The Plague*, and the ominous quiet of the primitive classroom high on an isolated plateau in "The

Guest," when the teacher, Daru, realizes that words are useless and
dialogue impossible. Silence, in short, is never merely physical or
aural. For Camus, it is also metaphysical and ethical. In the beginning was silence: the peace of a prelapsarian world. "All this noise,"
he wrote, "when peace would be to love and create in silence!"[24]
Just as in the scenes of the mother and son lying in silence, when
Camus seems to come full circle, first a newborn, then an adult, so
too in his travels. In an essay on a visit to Tipasa, an ancient site on
the Algerian coast, Camus describes finding "something which in
spite of time and in spite of the world was offered to me and truly
to me alone." From this something "not a sound came"; even the
sea "lay silent, as if breathless." In this silence, Camus understood
that he had returned to himself: "I felt I had come back to harbor,
for a moment at least, and that from now on this moment would
never end."[25]

But the moment does end, of course, leaving only a memory of
silence. As he leaves Tipasa, Camus reflects on this experience and
what it might mean. Silence bespeaks a world indifferent to politics and to others, while language is the work of a world of social
struggle and political engagement. The two worlds are equally vital,
but they are also opposed to each other. "There is beauty and there
are the humiliated," Camus insisted; he wishes to remain faithful to
both. Yet "this still sounds like ethics, and we live for something
that transcends ethics. If we could name it, what silence would
follow!"[26]

The interpretation of silence is, at best, an uncertain enterprise and, at worst, a fool's errand. Our situation is similar to that
of Camus when, as a child, he accompanied his illiterate grandmother to the cinema. It was the age of silent movies, and Camus
had to translate the subtitles for the old woman. It was an awkward
task: the child had to speak loudly enough so that his grandmother
could understand but softly enough not to disturb the others. He

also had to translate accurately enough to remain faithful to the story but quickly enough to keep up with the moving pictures. He managed this difficult job when it came to films like *The Mark of Zorro,* but other movies were just too complicated: "Caught between his grandmother's demands and the ever-angrier reprimands of his neighbors, [he] would end by remaining completely silent."[27]

Although some things cannot be named, they can still be shown. This brings us back, as it did Camus, to the image of his mother. Shortly before his death, he described his literary goal: to write a book at whose center would be "the admirable silence of a mother and one man's effort to rediscover a justice or a love to match this silence."[28] I am not sure what Camus meant by this claim. But Camus may not himself have fully understood what he meant. Perhaps this is how it should be: as Ludwig Wittgenstein said, while certain things cannot be said, particularly in the realm of ethics, this does not make them nonsensical or meaningless. We are stymied by the limits of language when we try to talk about the good because ethical propositions do not belong to the world of facts. But talk about the good we shall, talk about it we must. Wittgenstein declared that ethics, "so far as it springs from the desire to say something about the meaning of life, the absolute good, the absolute value, can be no science. What it says does not add to our knowledge in any sense. But it is a document of a tendency in the human mind which I personally cannot help respecting deeply and I would not for my life ridicule it."[29]

The contradiction at the heart of Camus's remark—namely, that the writer's effort to rediscover a justice or a love equal to his mother's silence forces him to speak—is also the contradiction at the heart of our own lives. We spend them looking for the right words in which to cast our greatest questions and deepest concerns. But final answers are not forthcoming—nor should we expect them to be. Instead, the continuous revision of our writing leads to a re-vision, a new vision, of what is most important in our lives. Iris Murdoch—a keen admirer of Camus's work—insisted that our "moral improvement is improvement of vision." Camus would certainly have agreed with this sentiment: from his earliest writings to the end of his life, he yoked himself to this task, his words plowing ever closer to the silences at the core of our lives and worlds.

CHAPTER ONE

1939

FROM COUNTY MAYO TO KABYLIA

Yes, there is beauty and there are the humiliated.
Whatever the difficulties the enterprise may present, I would
like never to be unfaithful either to one or the other.

Rarely had turn-of-the-century Ireland seemed so familiar as it did in interwar Algeria. The comic masterpiece by the early twentieth-century Irish playwright John Millington Synge, *The Playboy of the Western World,* had traveled to the edge of the Eastern world in 1939. An amateur theatrical group, the Théâtre de l'Equipe, was performing the play in the jewel of the French colonial crown, Algiers. But in unexpected ways, Synge's and the audience's worlds were similar. Both were impoverished margins of empires: French Algeria and British Ireland. Both were home to indigenous peoples, Irish Catholics and Arab Muslims, respectively, who were increasingly dissatisfied with foreign rule. Both were blasted by famine—resulting, in part, from imperial misrule—that forced great waves of immigrants to foreign shores. Both harbored ruling classes, the Anglo-Irish gentry and *pied noir* settlers, who were as much exiles in their adopted lands as they were in the mother countries. And both communities nurtured circles of artists who fought to express the experience of the colonized through the medium of the colonizer's language.

Albert Camus, the actor playing the role of Christy Mahon appreciated these parallels. In fact, Camus and Christy were kindred spirits. Like Camus's father, Lucien Camus, who had died in the Battle of the Marne in 1914, a year after the birth of his son, Old Mahon, Christy's father, had also been killed—or so his son thought. Christy had bashed him on the skull with a shovel, to discover days later that he had only knocked him unconscious. Both Camus and Christy had tongues that soared in flight, sweeping along women in their wake. (One can only imagine the reaction of one of the members of the amateur cast, Francine Faure, who would soon become Camus's second wife—and the victim of his serial infidelities—when Pegeen tells Christy that "any girl would walk her heart out before she'd meet a young man was your like for eloquence or talk at all.") Both men even shared the same heritage: Christy's background (or so he proclaimed) was in equal parts French and Spanish; the family of Camus's father hailed from Bordeaux (and not from Alsace, as Camus had always believed), and his mother's family came from Majorca.

And both men were still unformed. At the play's high point, when Christy learns Pegeen loves him, he wonders: "Is it me?" During the same period, though for different reasons, Camus also asked: "Is it me?" As he wrote in his journal: "I am uncertain of the future but have achieved total liberty toward my past and toward myself. Here lies my poverty, and my sole wealth. It is as if I were beginning the game all over again, neither happier nor unhappier than before. But aware now of where my strength lies, scornful of my own vanities, and filled with that lucid fervor which impels me forward toward my fate."[1]

o o o

In 1907, the opening of Synge's comedy in Dublin sparked a riot. Rather than the play's depiction of rural poverty, popular violence, or rough justice, the audience, according to some observers, had been shocked by an allusion to local women in their undergarments. While there were no riots at the Salle Pierre Bordes in 1939, poverty, violence, and justice were very much on the minds of the actors and audience that night. This was particularly true for Camus, the leader of the Théâtre de l'Equipe, the theatrical troupe responsible for the production. As he had already told one of his high school teachers, "I have such a strong desire to see reduced all the misfortune and bitterness which poisons humankind."[2] Camus echoed this sentiment in his journal: "I must bear witness," he insisted. "When I see things clearly, I have only one thing to say. It is in this life of poverty, among these vain or humble people, that I have most certainly touched what I feel is the true meaning of life."[3]

Between 1936 and 1939 both the Théâtre de l'Equipe and its predecessor, the Théâtre du Travail, were known as *la bande à Camus*. Veteran of a school production of Alexandre Dumas's *Three Musketeers*, Camus must have enjoyed the tag.[4] If it was a coincidence that he played the role of d'Artagnan, it was a happy one. Like the Gascon (and his compatriot, Cyrano de Bergerac), Camus was a young man from a region famed for its lyricism and courage. And as youthful and untried as d'Artagnan, Camus quickly imposed himself on the others as leader. Dumas's observation that it was "as if d'Artagnan had commanded others his entire life" applied equally to Camus.

No less important, d'Artagnan leads his fellow musketeers in their celebrated refrain: one for all and all for one. Since become a cliché, it nevertheless expressed more than simple romantic verve when exclaimed by friends united in a common enterprise. That refrain also underscores a dilemma at the heart of communitarian thought: How to reconcile individual initiative and group cohesion? Both theater groups insisted on equal participation between the actors and audience, just as they insisted on full parity among themselves. Yet, despite these official claims, Camus was clearly first among equals. He had founded both groups, influenced the choice of plays, directed the productions, and wrote his own works or adapted those of others. Yet this caused little dissension or resentment. One for all, all for one: these theatrical ventures sprang from Camus's conviction that theater must project the "collective realization of one man's thought."[5]

They also sprang from the idealism then sweeping through the French Left. As fascism threw its shadow across the continent during the 1930s, movements on the Left began to stir. In France, the formation of the Popular Front in 1934—the fragile alliance of Socialists, Communists, and Radicals—was spurred by a common fear of fascism at home. Though the Popular Front's time in power was short-lived, the idealism it nurtured was at the heart of Camus's theatrical work. It was a time when André Malraux's early novel, *L'âge du mépris* (Days of Contempt), portraying a working-class community's resistance to Nazism, was galvanizing French youth. The novel overwhelmed Camus. In fact, the young man was impressed enough to write to Malraux, asking for permission to adapt the story for the Théâtre du Travail. The older man, in turn, was impressed enough by the unknown writer's gumption that he sent a one-word reply: "Play." Camus was as overjoyed by the dramatic command as he was by the familiar *tu* form in which it was cast.

o o o

"André Malraux" was perhaps André Malraux's greatest dramatic creation: few figures in modern France were more gifted at representing themselves on the stage of history—or more driven to do so. By the time Camus entered university, he sympathized with this desire. When among friends, Camus reveled in playacting, miming scenes, declaiming speeches, mixing comedy and tragedy. (A bit like a North African Damon Runyon, he especially relished the patois and accents he heard in the streets and cafés of Algiers.) But as with his hero Malraux, the young *pied noir* often blurred the line between theater and reality, stage and street. Even when alone, he tended to see his life in theatrical terms. Commentators have, in fact, suggested that Camus turned himself into a character and director in his letters and writings: acting for Camus was "a fundamental form of existence."[6] How else to conceive a man who, in his journal, expressed the desire to be "the perfect actor"?

At first glance, this is a common human trait: we all try to make sense of ourselves by staging our lives. Many of us are old hands at such cognitive two-steps, when we stand outside ourselves, assuming the roles of director and commentator. For Camus, this habit became more frequent as he grew more famous. "I'm at my best at funerals. Really, I shine," he wrote with muted sarcasm in the early 1950s. "I walk slowly through iron-festooned suburbs, down wide lanes bordered by cement trees leading to holes dug in the cold ground. There, under a dimly red sky, I look on as stout fellows lower my friend six feet under. A clay-covered hand passes me a flower: I never miss when I toss it into the grave. I show the proper piety and emotions, my head tilted just right. To everyone's admiration, I find the right words. But I take no credit: I am waiting."[7]

Yet Camus mined this tendency in remarkable ways. His notebooks bristle with reflections, often contradictory, on authenticity and acting. On the one hand, he urged himself to be "deep through insincerity" and admired Eugène Delacroix's remark that the "illusions I create with my painting are the most real thing in me. The rest is shifting sand." Soon after he turned thirty, Camus declared that at this age a "man ought to have control over himself ... be what he is ... settle in to being natural, but with a mask."[8]

On the other hand, Camus blurred the line between sincerity and insincerity, mask and self. In a particularly complex passage he sketched in 1937 for *A Happy Death*, the character Patrice insists that "if the actor gave his performance without knowing that he was in a play, then his tears would be real tears and his life a real life. ... I am carried away by the knowledge that the game I am playing is the most exciting and serious there is." He adds after a pause: "And I want to be this perfect actor."[9]

Is the mask our natural self? Or instead, is there a natural self still intact behind the mask? Camus's thoughts reflect the concerns expressed two centuries before by Jean-Jacques Rousseau. So similar to the Swiss thinker in other respects, Camus here turns Rousseau on his head. In his *Letter to d'Alembert*, Rousseau famously damns theater: it is a surrogate for existence, a simulacrum of community, a sink of iniquity and falsehood. Acting, for Rousseau, was becoming the "fundamental form of existence" in the modern age—and this was precisely the problem. "When we do not live in ourselves but in others, it is their judgments which guide everything." The problem with theater, Rousseau declared, was that it gets in the way of life, coming between man and his world, between man and his own self. Theater is thus little more than modern life writ small. Instead of cultivating the virtues of citizenship and family, tragedians stage these virtues, replacing reality with appearance and lived experience with vicarious experience.

At first glance, Camus takes this "problem" and turns it into a solution: since we are condemned to act, let us act well and let us act together. While Rousseau believed it was only in solitude that

he could regain his own self, Camus, though he had an aptitude for
solitude, was convinced it was only in the company of others that
he could find or shape his self. "Seek contacts. All contacts," he
exhorted himself in 1936. "If I want to write about men, should I
stop talking about the countryside? If the sky or light attract me,
shall I forget the eyes or voices of those I love?"[10]

But Camus also wished that he could be the perfect actor. Did
he mean so perfect that he would become his role? Or so perfect
that his real self, standing to one side, could only admire the performance? It may well be that, for Camus, the "actor is the man
who incarnates unreality and hence he is the only true man."[11] Not
that Camus ever associated truth with unreality: he was too rooted
in the world's profane truths and beauties to ever believe that. But
if by "unreality" we understand only "art" or "artifice," we get
closer to the truth.

Camus does not say if he had ever read Rousseau's critique of
theater. If he had, however, he would have sided not with Rousseau but with Rousseau's friend become nemesis, Denis Diderot.
In his *Confessions*, Rousseau recounts a visit he made to the *philosophe*
at the prison of Vincennes. On entering Diderot's cell, Rousseau
threw himself into his friend's arms "with my face pressed against
his, speechless except for the tears and sobs that spoke on my behalf, for I was choked with tenderness and joy." When they finally
disengaged, Diderot triumphantly turned to another visitor: "Observe, Monsieur, how my friends love me!" Rather than wring his
hands over issues of sincerity, Diderot applauded the theatrics of
goodness, either at the Comédie Française or in a prison cell. It was
good to stage the good.

Camus, like Diderot, believed in the moral potential of theater.
This conviction helps explain the weakness of his theatrical pieces,
which are often mired in a kind of ethical didacticism. But this conviction also reveals Camus's great desire to connect with others: to

enter into a dialogue not just with his fellow actors but also with his audience. As Camus often repeated (but did not always practice in his own theatrical pieces), on "stage as in reality, the monologue precedes death."[12] Far from corrupting and enslaving us, Camus believed, theater could make us better and freer.

Becoming better and freer, however, depended on the audience. In its manifesto, the Théâtre du Travail declared it was "sometimes advantageous to art to descend from its ivory tower." To this end, the group decided, gate proceeds would go to a fund for unemployed workers in Algiers. Yet benighted crowds hungry for culture were not necessarily waiting at the tower's front door. Camus and his friends, determined to bring art to the people, discovered that the people were, by and large, much less determined to come to the art. While hundreds turned out for the performance, few of them were European or Arab workers. Instead, the spectators reflected the social character of Camus's gang: young, European, and bourgeois. And yet the play's impact on this small slice of the French Algerian community was immediate and important. As one spectator later recalled, they "saw unfold on stage our own struggle against the degrading mindset of fascism."[13]

This spirit of resistance also swept through the troupe's preparations for *Revolt in Asturias*, a collective work dramatizing an uprising of Spanish miners in 1934. The mayor of Algiers, Maximim Rozis, a member of the militant right movement Action Française, denied Camus's troupe permission to stage the work in the municipal theaters. The play was derailed, prodding a furious Camus into a relentless letter campaign against Rozis—among the gentler remarks he made was that "we can no longer say ridicule kills, since Rozis is still alive."[14] The Spanish Republicans had just engaged Franco's rebels in a slow, agonizing, and ultimately losing war. In many ways, the Spanish Civil War turned out to be a rehearsal for the "good war" soon to begin across the globe: one that pitted the forces of fascism against the forces of democracy. While the republic attracted dubious allies—first and foremost the Soviet Union—it also claimed the allegiance of groups and individuals committed to democratic and progressive ideals. Camus later placed the Spanish Civil War at the center of his personal history as well as world history. The bloody events in Spain were a "personal tragedy," but they were also his generation's tragedy: "Our history begins with this lost war and our true teacher has been Spain. She has taught us that history does not choose between just and unjust causes, and that it submits to sheer force when not to mere chance."[15]

○ ○ ○

Camus had the Spanish Civil War in common with an Englishman to whom he is often compared, George Orwell. Indeed, they shared the same disease as well. While fighting with the Republicans in 1936, a bullet tore through Orwell's throat, contributing to the tuberculosis that eventually killed him. Tuberculosis had found Camus long before that: he was scarcely seventeen when he had his first coughing fit in Algiers. One winter's day in 1930, the spasms grew so violent that Camus began to vomit blood. After being rushed to a local hospital, he was given a grim prognosis. On his release from the hospital, Camus told his Uncle Gustave, "I don't want to die."[16]

Though his stay at the hospital was short, his memory of it was long. In an unpublished fragment, titled "A Poor Neighborhood's Hospital," Camus offers a bleak sketch of a TB ward. One morning, a group of patients, "ugly and skeletal, their voices strangled from laughter and coughing," leaves the building to sit outside. After a while, one of them says to no one in particular, "The illness comes quickly, but leaves slowly."[17]

Tuberculosis did not kill Camus, but it subjected his body to a kind of foreign occupation for the rest of his life. Camus sometimes resisted, more often accommodated himself to the disease. He admired friends such as Robert Namia, who announced one evening that he was quitting the Théâtre de l'Equipe's rehearsals for *Hamlet*, for he had decided to go to Spain.[18] But Camus knew it was foolhardy to cross the Pyrenees. In 1936, the Spanish republic did not need foreign volunteers who could more easily spit their own blood than spill that of others.

By 1936, however, Camus had taken a step Orwell had always refused: he signed on with Communism. The preceding fall, he joined the French Communist Party (PCF). Here as elsewhere, Camus solicited the help of his high school literature teacher, Jean Grenier, to think through his decision. Grenier had suggested that Camus's energy might best be yoked to organized politics. Grenier had few illusions—a rarity at that time—about the radiant future projected by the PCF. In his lectures and essays—Grenier had a modest literary reputation in Paris, publishing from time to time in the country's most prestigious literary journal, *La Nouvelle Revue Française*—he warned against the unequal struggle between the life of ideas and political idealism. As he warned Camus, "each time man creates new values, he creates new shackles."[19] But he had equally few illusions about his protégé's desire to engage the world. Like so many others of his generation, Camus aspired "towards something that transcends the human."[20] The PCF, Grenier thought, might serve as a suitable, though temporary, place for Camus's moral convictions and political restlessness.

As a result, a teacher who distrusted messianic ideologies led his favorite student, who was immune to "ideal truths," to join a party embodying these very ideologies. To Grenier's curt question—"Should one, for an ideal of justice, accept stupid ideas?"—Camus answered "yes." His assent was short-lived: stupid ideas, Camus quickly understood, make for a stupid world. In his journal, Camus proudly described himself as an intellectual—in other words, "someone whose mind watches itself."[21] No less important, the intellectual attends not just to his own thoughts but to the lives of others. In a way, Camus inhabited his thought, no less than the lives of others, the way he inhabited a role on stage: with great energy and equally great critical distance.

It was an art of living that did not endear him to the local Communist apparatus. Along with questioning others no less than himself, Camus took to heart the party's egalitarian ethos. The PCF had had the great merit, unique among France's political parties, of taking seriously the miserable lot of the Arab and Berber populations. When Camus joined them in late 1935, French Communists had already established themselves as foes of French imperialism. The PCF demanded the political enfranchisement of Algeria's Muslim population, as well as their economic and social betterment. This was a truly revolutionary stance in a country where nine out of ten residents, all of them Arab or Berber, were politically excluded and economically exploited.

Camus's decision was neither sudden nor surprising. While still a high school student, he joined a weekly journal called *Ikdam*. Founded by the grandson of the nineteenth-century Algerian nationalist Abd al-Kadir, *Ikdam* demanded that the French republic live up to its ostensibly universalist credo. A nation founded on the rights of man and of the citizen must extend those same rights to the Arabs and Berbers under its rule. For these early Muslim nationalists, as for Camus, the official republican policy of assimilation was not a lie that cloaked the brutal reality of colonization— or, more accurately, it was neither simply nor inevitably a lie.[22] While French colonial policy was undeniably racist and paternalist, it was not only that. Infused with the universal and egalitarian sentiments of 1789, France's republican credo remained untouched by the racial and ethnic considerations that tainted the policies of other Western imperial powers. In that narrow space between the inspiring rhetoric of republicanism and the depressing reality of everyday racism, it was possible to believe that Algeria would always be fully French, fully republican, and fully free for *all* of its inhabitants. A generation of indigenous nationalist leaders—the interwar Algerian leader Ferhat Abbas is a notable example—as well as exceptional *pieds noirs* such as Camus all acted on the belief that France's role in the colonies was to lay the foundations for equality, not enslavement.[23] In the end, however, such men and women were too few in the face of the reality of institutional and popular racism. In this regard, it is telling that most proponents of assimilation did not direct their efforts at the indigenous peoples, whom they judged too barbaric, but instead at European immigrants to Algeria like Camus's own family.

Camus nevertheless joined in the last great effort to bring *pieds noirs* and Muslims under the same republican roof. In May 1937, the Algerian newspapers carried a manifesto whose aims, though in fact moderate, seemed absolutely revolutionary in the context of the times. In half a dozen terse paragraphs, the manifesto's fifty signers, including Camus, declared their support for the Blum-Viollette project. Proposed by the Popular Front prime minister Léon Blum and his representative in Algeria, Maurice Violette, the bill, which never became law, would have extended full political rights to more than twenty thousand Arabs and Berbers. For conservatives, it was too great a step, whereas nationalists dismissed it as too small. But for Camus, it was a necessary step in the right direction. A culture cannot survive without dignity, the manifesto stated, and a civilization cannot flourish under oppressive laws. How could one even speak of culture when an entire people is "deprived of schools" or of civilization when people are "bowed under unprecedented misery and humiliating laws"?[24]

The PCF supported the bill. Yet just months later, the party's leadership sacrificed its anticolonialism to strategic considerations. Joseph Stalin had decided that fascism represented a greater threat to the Soviet Union than did imperialism, and that Nazi Germany posed a greater danger than imperial France or England. Accordingly, Communist parties across the continent were ordered to mute their anticolonial rhetoric and instead turn their attention to the fascist threat. Camus refused to go along with this brutal instance of realpolitik. For him, the two struggles were complementary, not antagonistic. As he wrote to his friend and fellow Communist, Claude de Fréminville, "I will never place a copy of Marx's *Capital* between life and my fellow men."[25] By fellow men, Camus meant Arabs and Berbers no less than *pieds noirs.*

∘ ∘ ∘

As a student at the University of Algiers, Camus wrote his thesis on neo-Platonism and Augustine. The work is largely a concoction of secondary sources and unexceptional glosses, but it remained close to Camus's heart.[26] This may well be, in part, because he felt so close to his subject. Camus was fond of calling Augustine, who was born in what is now Libya, the "other North African." Augustine demanded that the world reveal an ultimate meaning, all the while wrestling with its sensual attractions. In his *Confessions*, Augustine recounts his great struggle with sexual desire and the unbearable tension between his love of God and his love of the carnal world. Nearly driven mad, he uttered his famous prayer, "Lord save me, but not just yet." Like Augustine, Camus was intensely aware of the power and pleasures of the physical world; like Augustine, he also knew that nature itself offers no lessons. But here they diverged: for Augustine, God alone has the answer; for Camus, however, man would have only questions.

In an important sense, Camus's passage through the PCF resembled Augustine's experience with Manichaeanism. No other belief system, he thought, better explained the character of our lives. The Manichees affirmed the existence of two antagonistic entities, Good and Evil, one associated with light, the other with darkness or matter. These two principles, they said, have been locked in a battle since the beginning of time, climaxing with the advent of Jesus Christ. A deep desire courses through this belief system: to salvage those elements of light that have been imprisoned and sullied by the physical world. From the moment of the fall, man *and* god have struggled to regroup and purify themselves. In short, human beings are no longer mere subjects of history, they are now cast as actors.

Manichaeanism thus offered a rational conception of God steeped in the saving passion of Christianity. It was a cult of redemption, but expressed with greater intellectual rigor than Christian apologetics. How better to reconcile the existence of evil and the fragility of goodness than by asserting that they were two universal impulses at war with each other? No less important, the Manichees satisfied a young man's thirst for action and his desire to fight on behalf of the good. And so the young Augustine, desperate for meaning and engagement, joined the Manichees. Yet he was never at home with them: their rigid approach failed, in the end, to offer the answers he demanded. After several years, he finally left, restless and unsatisfied, and ultimately converted to Christianity.

Camus was equally ill at ease with the Communists. While the party allowed the young man to work on behalf of a future "good" for all humankind, it did not tolerate members who questioned party dogma. When the local cell was told to tar their former allies, Algerian nationalists, as fascist lackeys, all in the interest of this ideological good, Camus protested. After all, one of his duties had been the recruitment of Arab members: to repudiate this activity, he felt, was morally and politically wrong. Though the local leadership, in particular Amar Ouzegane, sympathized with Camus's rebelliousness, their flexibility was limited. In November 1937 Camus was expelled from the party—a formality, really, since he had already gone his own way. He would not abandon the Algerian Arabs, even if others insisted that the train of History was pulling out of the station without him.

o o o

The PCF was impressed by Camus's theatrical activities and had hoped to harness this energy for their cause. For Camus, too, theater had been, in part, politics by other means. But acting did not pay the bills, particularly after Camus cut his ties with the PCF. As a result, he sought other avenues that would allow him to write and earn a living at the same time. It is during this same period that he established ties with a local newspaper, *Alger-Républicain*, which was launched in late 1937 as a counterweight to Algiers's two conservative newspapers. The life of *Alger-Républicain* was bold, short, and desperate, the perfect vehicle for a young man with few prospects and great ambitions. Like Camus's theater troupes, *Alger-Républicain* was politically engaged but unattached to a political party or platform. And just as Camus's theatrical productions refused to subordinate artistic concerns to ideological claims, *Alger-Républicain* placed truth ahead of political convictions. Such, at least, was its claim in its stirring manifesto: insisting that the paper's sole concern was the "public interest," the editors made clear that, by "public," they meant *all* the inhabitants of French Algeria: the paper was as opposed to an "anti-Semitism made in Germany" as it was to social policies "aimed at keeping our indigenous friends in a position of inferiority." The newspaper insisted on full social and political equality for all Frenchmen "regardless of their race, religion, or philosophy."[27]

These admirable sentiments had a limited audience in interwar Algiers. The number of *Alger-Républicain* readers was never commensurate with the newspaper's fervor. Moreover, for reasons of economy, the paper's editor, Pascal Pia, staffed the newsroom with absolute beginners who were willing to work for a pittance. As much an amateur here as on the stage, Camus nevertheless leaped at the opportunity—to Pia's great satisfaction: "He never said anything insignificant," Pia later recalled about his rookie reporter, "yet he expressed himself plainly."[28]

At first, however, Camus dismissed his work as insignificant. His assignments, he told Grenier, boiled down to reporting about dogs hit by cars: "You know better than I do how disappointing this profession has been." Yet Camus also found it compelling. He felt free: "I don't feel constrained and everything I do seems alive."[29] He eventually found the platform offered by the newspaper as compelling as his theatrical activities. In December 1938, Camus filed the first story that carried his byline, a visit to a prison ship docked at Algiers. As Camus walked toward the ship on this cold, wet, and windswept day, he saw three Arabs, faces pressed to one of the portholes, gazing silently at Algiers. Unlike their fellow French prisoners, who were now "strangers in a strange world," these three men seemed to be searching for "something of themselves in the rain." As for the reporter, he makes no effort to maintain critical distance: "I'm not very proud to be here."

As he boarded the ship, steeling himself for an official tour no doubt meant to convey the reach and majesty of impartial justice, Camus worried about his dripping raincoat. Its damp scent, redolent of the outside world, was the last thing these men needed. As he prepared to leave the hold, he writes, "one of the prisoners asks me in Arabic for a cigarette." Camus knew it was against the rules but did not say so to the prisoner. That would have been such a "ludicrous reply," Camus realizes, for someone seeking "a sign of complicity, a fellow man's gesture." And yet, Camus did not respond to the man, instead meeting the request with silence. Only after he left the ship did he realize that he was seized not by pity but by something different and deeper: "There is no sight more dismal than that of men who have become less than human." Camus cannot escape the sight of men for whom the clammy odor of a winter's day in Algiers is proscribed. His one wish is to convey "the singular fate of men who have been struck from humanity."[30]

With the "Hodent affair" in 1939, Camus acted to prevent yet another such "singular fate" from befalling one man. Michel Hodent was a minor French bureaucrat who, despite the hostility of his superiors, tried to help poor Arab farmers living in his jurisdiction. Trumped-up charges were made against him, leading to a hasty trial and imprisonment. In a series of articles for *Alger-Républicain* during the spring of 1939, Camus attacked the state's case against Hodent. His repeated references to a suspicious *bordereau*, the meticulous dissection of the testimony and evidence, the use of an "open letter" to the authorities, and the repeated appeals to justice all recall the language of "J'accuse," Emile Zola's celebrated defense of Alfred Dreyfus fifty years before. But with a difference: Zola focused largely on an abstract notion of justice, while Camus attends to the injustice done to a single man. The worst crimes become possible, Camus warned, when we refuse to see men as men. This conviction appears early in Camus's notebooks: "My whole effort, whatever the situation, misfortune or disillusion, must be to make contact again."[31] Camus latches on to this moral imperative in a closing plea to the governor general. "We have glimpses of you in processions, laws, and speeches," he tells the official in his open letter. But "where do we find the man in all of that?" Behind the stage set and scenery, it "happens that the man appears." Camus appeals to this flesh-and-blood man on behalf of another man: to save the life of an individual "in a world where the humanity of so many others is lost to absurdity and misery…amounts to saving oneself."[32] Hodent was eventually released.

Later that year, Camus tried to provoke another "affair" with his series of reports on the trial of twelve Arab farmhands accused of arson. The fires had broken out during a strike begun by Arab workers: they were protesting a daily wage—four to six francs— that scarcely allowed them to live. The fires burned down a handful of hovels, and there was no evidence of the men's guilt. Instead, the dozen men confessed to the crime only after the police tortured them—waterboarding happened to be the preferred method. They each faced five years of hard labor if found guilty by the jurors. And all twelve men were fathers; their families, Camus noted, would be left without their principal wage earner.

For Camus, these men were guilty only of speaking the truth: they "dared say that their salary did not suit their dignity as men."[33] As a result, the trial's sole purpose was to warn others against acting on the same impulse. If Arab workers insisted on being treated as human beings, they would pay a very high price. Yet, if "democracy had any meaning at all, we will find it here and not in the official boilerplate" offered by elected officials. Camus asked the jurors to recall that, in the ritual address to the court made before delivering their verdict, they would declare that they were speaking "in the name of the French people." But this, Camus warned, would be "a lie" if followed by a guilty verdict.[34]

After his success in the Hodent affair, Camus now tasted failure. His articles did not save the twelve men: they were found guilty and punished. Yet these were trials in more than the judicial sense of the word: for Camus, they were also trials, essays, in ethical imagination. Just as Zola became Zola in the crucible of the Dreyfus affair—becoming the public figure we recognize today—so too did Camus become Camus during these journalistic affairs. They honed not just his language but also his appreciation for the vast gap between French ideals and imperial rule in Algeria. Camus hammered at the prejudices of his fellow *pieds noirs*, the hypocrisy and fecklessness of most local officials; he demanded a French Algeria equal to its republican values. As he declared after a similar event, when the government imprisoned several Muslim nationalists: "If only this was simply a stupid and incredibly narrow-minded policy that misunderstands the great power exercised by martyrs. But such actions are also deadly for France's reputation and future. If there ever was an anti-French politics, it is in the policy of our government."[35] In other words, France was falling short of its own history and values. This would be fatal, Camus held, but it was not fated. It was not a matter of "exalting the French empire but of making it," he wrote, adding, "it will never be made against its own subjects."[36] This truth was made clear during his visit that spring to the region of Kabylia.

o o o

"The final and most revolting injustice is consummated when poverty is wed to the life without hope or the sky I found on reaching manhood in the appalling slums of our cities....Though born poor in a working class neighborhood, I never knew what real misfortune was until I saw our chilly suburbs. Even extreme Arab poverty cannot be compared to it, because of the difference in climate."[37] Camus's lyricism here gets the better of him. Famine did not strike the urban poor in France, but even the blinding Algerian sun could not hide the fact that, during the 1930s, its people were dying of starvation in Kabylia.

East of Algiers, a jagged line forms the horizon: it is the Djurdjura, the craggy mountain range of Kabylia. Though a short distance from the capital city, Kabylia could have been, for most of the city's European residents, on another planet. The land was arid, seamed by valleys pocked with fig and olive orchards, and farmed by Berbers whose mountaintop villages seemed nearly hermetic, bare walls blindly facing the outside world, with windows and doors opening inward.

Assemblies of elders governed village life in Kabylia—a mark of primitive equality for some observers, a sign of patriarchal power for others. (As first among equals in the Théâtre de l'Equipe, Camus must have been attracted to both aspects.) This form of self-governance helped make it the last region in Algeria to be "pacified" by the French. Paradoxically, when Napoleon III fell from power in France in 1871, the future narrowed rather than widened for the Berbers. The most powerful shield for the native peoples of Algeria had been Napoleon's empire: imperial officials long tried to contain the greed of European settlers. But as post-Napoleonic France groped its way toward a republican form of government, the *pieds noirs* rushed to stake their claims in Kabylia. When the Berbers resisted, the local authorities unleashed the military that, in turn, performed as successfully and bloodily as their counterparts had against the Paris Commune.

The settlers completed the process they had begun, confiscating land and exacting heavy tributes from the Berber tribes. The arable valleys, which could scarcely support the people already trying to scratch out a living there, were taken by settlers, who had been given carte blanche by the local administration. Pushed out of the valleys, the Berbers either returned to their mountain villages or emigrated to metropolitan France, just as Irish peasants went to England. The Berbers were also subjected to a regime of exceptional laws, known as the *code de l'indigénat.* It was illegal for them to speak disrespectfully to French officials, defame the government, or travel without an official permit. Most ironic, the republic revived the feudal practice of the *corvée:* the local population became an unpaid and unwilling labor pool for European landowners. Despite its unforgiving soil, Kabylia thus welcomed the seeds of revolution: as one local poet wrote, the French "have sowed hatred in the villages / We store it under the ground where it remains / The abundant yield of a harvested field."[38]

o o o

"When one reaches the first slopes of Kabylia, catching sight of small villages huddled near the summits, the men draped in white woolen robes, the paths bordered by olive trees, fig trees and cactus, the simplicity of life and landscape, man and earth, one cannot help but think of Greece."[39] Or at least, the narrator cannot help but think of Greece, forcing on us the unexpected comparison in order to undo our preconceptions about Algeria. In the opening lines of his first report from Kabylia, dated June 5, 1939, Camus culls references and images from picturesque accounts of Kabylia written by other European visitors. They are exotic but recognizable—the narrative equivalent of a Club Med vacation.

For that matter, they are like the stage sets of commercial theater—overdone and predictable—so despised by Camus's theatrical muse, Jacques Copeau. During the interwar period, Copeau, the celebrated director of the Théâtre du Vieux Colombier, rebelled against the bourgeois traditions of French theater. Rather than cultivating lush stage scenery and actors all too eager to chew on it, Copeau stripped his productions bare: everything and everyone were yoked to the written word.

Camus carefully read Copeau's essays in the *Nouvelle Revue Française*, the same journal to which Jean Grenier contributed. The Parisian director showed Camus how the unreality of theater can be made to serve as a reality check. The stage, Copeau insisted, must be as "empty and as bare as possible [and] shaped by the unfolding of a story: such a set is most beautiful in its natural state, primitive and vacant."[40] In the opening passage of "Misery in Kabylia," Camus, like Copeau, pushes away the traditional décor. And like him, Camus banishes familiar stage settings: "But let it be said now: this land's misery is overwhelming."[41] The snow-frosted slopes, already opening to ski resorts; the quaint local practices, always a familiar opening for a forgettable tale, all dissolve. Camus instead marshals his actors, Berber men, women, children; he reveals the script they have been dealt, a litany of despair and agony; and he allows the story to tell itself.

Two years earlier, Camus had already drafted the opening to his reports from Kabylia. In October 1937, he had made a camping trip to the region. Like Sisyphus, Camus pushed his own burden, tubercular lungs, up and down the barren hills, noting the "concentrated effort of walking uphill, the air burning my lungs like a red-hot iron or cutting into them like a sharpened razor." His labored breathing did not stop him from seeing this world: Camus reports on the villages, flora, and inhabitants. The ties between Kabylia and Greece filled his thoughts. Marveling at the rough land, Camus kept being drawn back to Greece. But no, he reminded himself: he was abroad at home, he was in Kabylia. Here lies the critical difference: in the *Notebooks*, he maintained the parallel—it is as if "the whole of Greece had suddenly been set down between the sea and mountains, reborn in its ancient splendor"—whereas the title of his first article in *Alger-Républicain*, "Greece in Rags," makes the comparison only to demolish it. The recent, catastrophic harvests, coupled with the administration's inertia and the indifference of the *pieds noirs*, led Camus to mock the earlier parallels he himself had made.[42]

Camus overturns other inevitable invocations of the picturesque. At dusk, he climbed with a Berber companion—Camus stayed with friends during his visit, most of whom were Berber schoolteachers—to a hill overlooking the town of Tizi-Ouzou.

For a moment, he wrote, he was carried away by the starry sky and grand vistas. Then he spied fires dotting the slopes: a scene seemingly resonant with ancient Greeks at one with the world. But he suddenly recalls the purpose of the fires: starving villagers used them to bake pancakes made from rotten oats. His companion then breaks the silence: "Shall we go down?"[43]

At the start, Camus announces his method: "I will use a minimum of words to describe what I saw."[44] The barer the stage, the clearer the text; the clearer the text, the sharper the moral meaning. In an important sense, for Camus, the moral landscape was as "real," as brute, as the physical landscape of North Africa. The two landscapes are, in fact, entwined. In 1937, he had already begun to stake out a "Mediterranean nationalism," one that embraced "physical life [and not] reasoning and abstractions."[45] Truths were rooted in the desert and coasts; they were concrete, tactile, elemental. "Between this sky and the faces turned toward it there is nothing on which to hang a mythology, a literature, an ethic, or a religion—only stones, flesh, stars, and those truths the hand can touch."[46] Or, in the case of the Berbers, it is "wheat, bread, and a brotherly hand: the rest is only words."[47]

Yet words scarcely sufficed for what Camus saw in Kabylia; it was certainly beyond anything he had imagined. He knew, for example, that the official distribution of grain did not meet the needs of the population. "But what I did not know is that these shortages were killing people."[48] In spare language, Camus depicted the horrifying reality of villages where malnourished children played by open sewers, fainted from hunger in classrooms, fought with dogs over kitchen scraps, were racked with convulsions, and died from eating poisonous roots. The absolute wretchedness of everyday life undermined the standard excuse of imperial apologists: all of this was due to the Berber "mentality," the bundle of local traditions and customs that threw a wall between these primitive souls and France's civilizing mission. Nonsense, replied Camus. It was a question of water, food, roads, and schools—all of which Kabylia sorely lacked and which the French authorities did not supply.

Camus dispatched a dozen articles from Kabylia, all of them carrying the same message: the misery of these human beings must not be obscured by "glib phrases or meditations. It is. It cries for our attention, it despairs of getting it."[49] Camus attended to this cry of despair in two different yet overlapping registers: political and ethical. In political terms, his despair was especially deep, if only because of the gap between the ideals of the French republic and the reality of Kabylia. Camus nevertheless insisted on the relevance of the republican ideal for Kabylia's predicament. There was nothing glib or self-righteous in his emphasis on education: instead, the student of Louis Germain spoke from the heart. The practice of separate and unequal education had to end. The classroom had to be integrated: the people of Kabylia, Camus wrote, will have "more schools the day we do away with the artificial barriers separating the European and indigenous systems of education." Only then, by sitting at the same desks, will "two peoples made to live together come to know each other."[50] Let us focus, he said, on the bonds of fraternity, not the barriers of difference that existed between the two peoples. If France believed in its policy of assimilation, if it believed Muslims were truly worthy of being French, then "we cannot begin by separating them from us."[51] In the end, for Camus, France had to practice, not simply preach, republicanism—the ideology that rendered France's imperial heritage so problematic but also so promising. If France's "colonial conquests were ever to find their justification, it is to the degree that it allows the conquered peoples to keep their identities. If we have but one duty in this country, it is to permit a people so proud and humane to remain true to itself and its destiny."[52]

Camus assumed the Berber destiny would dovetail with that of France: a naïve claim, perhaps. Equally naïve, for some, was his belief that seeing was believing—and that believing would lead to practical policy. Camus wrote that if the deputies of the French National Assembly, regardless of political affiliation, took the same itinerary he had taken in Kabylia, the solution would be at hand. But was this belief naïve? It underscored, of course, Camus's allegiance to the universal bonds of fraternity embodied by the republic. More important, however, it flowed from a simple, but not simplistic, ethical orientation: seeing rightly is a prerequisite to acting rightly. Camus recounted a visit he makes to a *gourbi,* or hut, in the village of Adni. In a "dim and smokey room, I was welcomed by two women, one quite aged, the other pregnant. Three children stare uncomprehendingly at me.... I don't see a single piece of furniture. Only after my eyes grow accustomed to the darkness do I see signs of human life: three great basins of white clay, and two earthen bowls." When Camus asks the pregnant woman, who is "cradling her enormous stomach," where she slept, she "pointed to the earthen floor under my feet, next to a drain serving as toilet."[53]

Camus does not ask the reader to enter this woman's head—he himself cannot do it, though he is standing there, in the darkened room where "animal odors and smoke grip [his] throat." Instead, he can do no more than step *next* to her—next to the open pit serving as a toilet, next to her swollen belly, next to three famished children—and pay attention. As Michael Walzer notes, we do not enter someone's head when we step into their shoes. "To think that we do is a characteristic mistake of philosophers who believe that heads have no histories. We don't, because we can't, reproduce other people's ideas; instead, we reiterate our own. But the recognition that the others have experiences and ideas similar to ours is already a significant moral achievement."[54]

Camus made a near identical point: we always take a step forward, he wrote, when we substitute a human problem for a political problem.[55] For better or worse, he offered no grand theoretical frame for his claim. But he did not believe he needed to: moral outrage was the work of experience, not theory; hatred of injustice is the result of a life lived, not a book opened.

o o o

Camus's embrace of his era's responsibilities had immediate consequences, personal and political. Three days after Camus's last dispatch from Kabylia, *La Dépêche Algérienne*, a conservative newspaper with close ties to Mayor Rozis—who had earlier prevented Camus's troupe from staging *Revolt in Asturias*—launched a series of articles written by a house journalist, R. Frison-Roche. Titled "Kabylie 39," the articles try to undo the damage done by Camus's reports. At the very start, Frison-Roche makes clear his position on the benefits of French imperialism: "The work France has accomplished here in less than a century would strike the most obtuse visitor."[56] Obtuseness, it seems, was not Camus's only flaw: Frison-Roche also suggests that his (unnamed) colleague was blinded by ideology. The misery of the Berbers was not the result of unfeeling French administrators, he declares, but of the grim Malthusian math afflicting Kabylia: there are too many mouths to feed, too many people crowded onto too little land. Infrastructure, land distribution, water access, education, and grain distribution: these subjects, to which Camus gave so much attention, are mostly ignored by Frison-Roche. Instead, time and again, he celebrates "the great and beautiful things France has done in Kabylia."[57]

Alger-Républicain welcomed the controversy: How else could the struggling newspaper win publicity? But all the controversies in the world could not save Pia and Camus's paper from its continued financial difficulties and the growing material constraints under which it was now placed. France had just lurched into war against Germany, but even before the declaration of war in September, the local government had targeted political movements it considered insufficiently patriotic. Both the Communist Party and the nationalist Algerian People's Party (PPA) were outlawed, its leaders imprisoned, and its rank and file harassed. The government's violence and shortsightedness stunned Camus: "It is not martyrs we need to make, but free and respected citizens." As the number of political martyrs grew, so too would the number of Algerian nationalists.

Camus again invoked this simple political calculus in the wake of a bloody police action at a PPA rally in mid-August. He could not decide which was worse: the moral baseness of the action or its political stupidity. Such activities, he warned, were as "damaging for France's prestige as they are for its future. If there ever was a true anti-French politics, it is revealed in these events." Camus demanded the release of the imprisoned demonstrators, declaring with a lucidity that only now seems commonplace, "We will not stamp out the claims of the indigenous peoples by passing over them in silence, but by examining them in a spirit of generosity and justice. The only way in which we can eradicate Algerian nationalism is by suppressing the injustices from which it is born."[58]

The following month, it was Alger-Républicain's turn to be hounded by the government. Government censors were installed in the newspaper's offices, assigned the task of guaranteeing the newspaper's patriotic moxie: as the governor general told the paper's shareholders, "We're at war, que diable! I'm counting on your patriotism."[59] Camus lampooned this justification, finding it as dubious when applied to France's war effort as to its civilizing mission: the republic's well-being could be served only by truth, not by lies and censorship. "I am foolish enough to believe," he wrote after the government announced its first wave of press laws, "that in order to defend democracy, we must strengthen democratic practices. We cannot seek peace through dictatorial means."[60] Camus was particularly disturbed by the vagueness of the press laws: the fewer the details, the greater the encroachment on freedom of speech. These laws, he declared, "permit everything, authorize everything, and threaten everybody."[61]

The unequal battle between *Alger-Républicain* and the censors entered its endgame as France's "phony war" with Germany stretched into winter. Blank patches pocked the pages, the fruit of the censors' rejection of specific articles and of Camus's refusal to fill them with patriotic boilerplate. And as the staff withered as a result of the tightening budget and military call-ups, Camus began to resemble the sole defender of a fort who runs from post to post to give the enemy the impression they are facing a great force. He signed some articles with pseudonyms, published others anonymously, and reprinted passages from classical French writers, daring the censors to find fault with the patriotism of Victor Hugo or Pierre Corneille. Still other passages he refused to identify, luring the censors into an ambush. Camus once confronted his uniformed tormentors with an article they had rejected: "Messieurs," he announced, "it's by Montaigne. The name was omitted. Shall we really strike it out?"[62] This was so much more than a game of cat and mouse, however. Seizing a rare opportunity to write under his own name, Camus pinpointed the fundamental values at stake: "In our time the press is a terrifying weapon in the hands of those who control it. It makes and unmakes public opinion, it provokes, it restrains, and it exasperates. A well-known statesman once said that all he needed to lead the country to war was to wage a six-week press campaign. He was absolutely right."[63]

On New Year's Day 1940, Camus began his editorial by noting the annual tradition of wishing others the very best in the future. The problem with this tradition, he added, was that it *was* a tradition: "The fact that we renew these wishes every year shows that they are perfectly useless." And yet, Camus offered a wish: "We must not forget. If it is true that forgetting is a bit like consenting, than we must not sleep. Let us remain vigilant and never turn our eyes away from this bitter reality that overwhelms and crushes us.... But our sole greatness is in this struggle against forces greater than us. It is not our happiness we should now seek, but instead this sort of desperate greatness."[64] Little more than a week later, the authorities shut down *Alger-Républicain.*

o o o

At the end of *Playboy of the Western World,* a young man, hesitant and uncertain, with an uncertain past and an unpromising background, blossoms into self-confident maturity. At the end of a physically taxing visit to Kabylia, a twenty-six-year old *pied noir,* with but a handful of published essays to his credit and the first steady job of his life, as a journalist, blossomed into the confident observer and writer who, with a few colleagues, refused to submit to government pressure when not to do so bordered on treason.

But confident though he had become, Camus remained *mal dans sa peau*—uneasy in his skin. As he stood inside the Kabylian hovel at Adni, Camus felt the same shame he had known on the prison ship: "I must say I wasn't proud of myself." The journalist was so uneasy that he asked the woman just one question: Where did she and her children sleep? This kind of moral discomfort, this unease in the face of suffering, this malaise that pushes you to silence, hindered as much as it helped Camus. He wrote quickly, he wrote well, but he would have preferred writing on dogs flattened by cars in Algiers than on dogs fighting over bones with children in Tizi-Ouzou.

But his life as a journalist helped make Camus a moralist. A moralist, unlike a professional philosopher, is ill at ease in the world.

He is a truth teller, one whose truths make not only others feel uneasy but oneself as well: "To be a moralist was to lead an unquiet life—which is precisely what distinguished a moralist from an intellectual, whose public anguish over affairs of ethics or state normally accompanied an easy and confident private conscience."[65]

Did the young Camus welcome such a vocation? What would he have made of the other reason for the Dublin riots over *The Playboy of the Western World*? The reference to Irishwomen in their undergarments, it turns out, was just part of the problem. The rioters were also Irish chauvinists who were outraged by Synge's comic depiction of an Ireland inhabited by foul-mouthed and superstitious villagers who give a hero's welcome to a parricide. Synge hardly knew what to say in reply: "I wrote the play because it pleased me."[66] In an increasingly nationalistic era, however, Synge's caustic depiction of Ireland, or his justification, just did not sit well.

Camus would have sympathized, torn as he was between art and politics, the sensual beauty of the world and the heart-sickening misery of its human inhabitants. As he himself noted, "In everything I've done or said so far, I seem to recognize these two forces, even when they contradict one another. I have not been able to deny the light into which I was born and yet I have not wished to reject the responsibilities of our time."[67] With these two imperatives balanced uneasily on his shoulders, Camus left for Paris in 1939. The government had helped ensure that no one in Algiers would hire him.

CHAPTER TWO

1945

A MORALIST ON THE BARRICADES

Paris-Algiers. The airplane as one of the elements of modern negation and abstraction. There is no more nature; the deep gorge, true relief, the impassable mountain stream, everything disappears. There remains a *diagram*—a map. Man, in short, looks through the eyes of God. And he perceives then that God can have but an abstract view. This is not a good thing.

Liberated six months earlier, Paris in January 1945 was still burdened by the same shortages that had existed when it was ruled by the Germans. Heating fuel was scarce, food was even scarcer, and the black market flourished. The daily Parisian calorie intake hovered at one thousand, and the Provisional Government under General Charles de Gaulle was unable to retire the ration cards introduced by the Vichy regime. A three hundred–gram loaf of bread perhaps tasted sweeter in a free city than in an occupied one, but it still weighed only three hundred grams. That winter, the *New Yorker* journalist Janet Flanner wrote from Paris, "Nourished by liberation, warmed by the country's return to active battle, France is still physically living largely on vegetables and mostly without heat."[1]

One of the few things the straitened and shivering capital had in excess that winter was moral righteousness. The confidence to identify right and wrong, the assurance to distinguish innocence from guilt, and the strength to reward and punish was not just the grim yield of war against a foreign enemy. It was also the bitter harvest of a civil war waged between those who had resisted and those who had collaborated. As Camus asked, "Since the spirit finally understood that a sword is needed to conquer a sword, and since the spirit took up the sword and attained victory, who would ask it to forget?"[2] Camus had asked the question in the wake of liberation. But less than half a year passed before he began to question the rhetorical flourish. The problem was not that liberated France had been asked to forget the past. Instead, for Camus, the problem was what it had chosen to remember.

∘ ∘ ∘

After its shocking military victory over France in 1940, Germany occupied the northern, mostly urban and industrialized, half of the country, establishing its headquarters in Paris. France's southern half, largely rural and agricultural, was placed under the rule of the new French regime that had overthrown the defeated and discredited Third Republic. Unable to return to Paris, France's new rulers set up shop in the spa town of Vichy, whose many hotels and resorts were transformed into government ministries, and whose name has ever since been associated with this regime.

It soon became clear that "Vichy" was shorthand for the politics of collaboration. Rather than confining themselves to the essentials of administration, Vichy's leaders—most notably Philippe Pétain and Pierre Laval—were determined to earn a prominent place in Hitler's new European order. As Pétain declared shortly after meeting Hitler in October 1940, France had "entered on the path of collaboration." The path was paved by reactionary intentions: Vichy's ambition was to undo the egalitarian and enlightened legacy of France's republican past. The French Revolution's trinity of values—liberty, fraternity, equality—was replaced by Vichy's trilogy of work, family, and fatherland. The republic was buried and its place taken by an authoritarian state dedicated to the proposition that all men are not created equal: France would no longer welcome what one of the regime's heroes, the writer Charles Maurras, called *les anti-Frances.* The most vulnerable of these "foreign" bodies was French Jewry.

The German occupation and Vichy's collaborationist policies spurred the growth of the Resistance, a term of convenience for a complex phenomenon that encompassed a dizzying array of rebels and revolutionaries. Ranging from Communists to progressive Catholics, trade unionists to priests, nationalist military officers to Jewish academics, the Resistance was united by the desire to rid France of its German occupiers and bring French collaborators to justice. They generally used the "weapons of the weak"—spying and sabotage—and published underground newspapers, tracts, poems, and novels that nurtured the spirit of resistance.

These otherwise diverse and contradictory resistance movements were united as much in their distaste for Vichy's agenda as in their belief that France's liberation was just the first step. Of course, France had to rid itself of the German occupiers, but also of the tainted and unsavory politics practiced before the war. The young men and women of the Resistance did not risk their lives to resurrect the Third Republic. Instead, they demanded politics in a new key, cleansed of the political and ideological compromises practiced by their fathers, freed of their era's glaring economic and social disparities. Rebellion against Germany was the necessary prelude to a revolution against France's own recent history, a revolution based on a humanistic and universalist conception of man. Mere *politique* was shunned; there now was an overwhelming desire to live a certain kind of *mystique.*

This sentiment was broadcast in the first issue of the Resistance newspaper *Combat* to be published openly, on August 21, 1944. That day, Paris, no longer occupied, was still not yet free. The streets echoed with the clatter of gunfire exchanged between German soldiers and French resistance fighters, ending an uneasy truce concluded between the two sides the day before. Yet paperboys ran past the barricades and the shuttered storefronts, carrying copies of *Combat* emblazoned with its motto, "From Resistance to Revolution." The readers were told to brace for an even more difficult struggle in the coming months—one fought not against the Germans but among themselves. "The liberation of Paris is only one step toward the liberation of France, and here the word LIBERATION must be taken in its broadest sense....It will not be enough to return to the mere appearance of liberty with which the France of 1939 had to be content....The Allies have made our liberation possible. But our freedom is our own; it is we who must shape it."[3] Though the editorial was unsigned, its author was the newspaper's thirty-year old editor, Albert Camus.

∘ ∘ ∘

War-scarred Paris was far removed from Le Panelier, a farm in the Vivarais, a mountainous region of southeastern France. The soil was rocky and unforgiving, the villages far-flung and isolated, the inhabitants closed and stern. It was to Le Panelier that Camus and his wife, Francine, moved in early 1942. They had pressing reasons to do so: Camus had been stricken with a brutal recurrence of tuberculosis; the dry mountain air, doctors counseled, was vastly preferable to Algeria's humidity and heat. In the midst of occupation and war, such voyages required a good deal of paperwork; it was only in August that they were able to board a steamer to France. During his first few months in Le Panelier, Camus appreciated the severe beauty of the region; he compared the sweep of fir trees cascading along the mountainous slopes to a "barbarian army" that, he hoped, would "drive out the fragile army of nocturnal thoughts."[4] The land, seamed by deep valleys strewn with boulders and dotted with hamlets built by lean and laconic villagers, resembled the region of Kabylia on which Camus had reported just a few years before.

But it was difficult to keep dark thoughts at bay in October. Just as the weather was turning wet and cold, Francine returned to Oran and her teaching position. Alone and weak, Camus noted how the pinecones in his fireplace seemed like "infernal diamonds" with the "wind moaning about the house." From the window of the train he rode to the nearby city Saint-Etienne, where he went for lung treatment, Camus watched the peasants walking "bent forward, against the wind and rain." But far better these sights than what he found in Saint-Etienne, a grim industrial town that filled Camus with disgust and despair. As the train pulled into the station one morning, Camus glimpsed the "jumble of towers, buildings, and tall chimneys belching toward a darkened sky their deposit of cinders": the billowing cloud of ashes, he thought, looked "like a monstrous artificial cake."[5]

Worse was to come, however. On November 11, 1942, the Germans replied to the Allied landings in North Africa by crossing the Demarcation Line, which divided the Free and Occupied Zones established in 1940, and laying claim to the rest of France. That same day, Camus jotted in his notebook: "Caught like rats!" A wall had unexpectedly been thrown up between Camus and Algeria: he could no longer return to his family, friends, and familiar land-scapes. At the same time, the turn of events—his sudden and un-expected exile to an obscure village—concentrated his mind. The author of the recently published novel *The Stranger* now became his own most severe critic and revisited his first novel's portrayal of man's "absurd" lot.

Gallimard, the most prestigious publisher in Paris,, had brought out the book in 1942. On reading Camus's manuscript, André Mal-raux had immediately sent it to Jean Paulhan, the éminence grise at Gallimard. At the next editorial board meeting, Paulhan read aloud the novel's first lines—"Mama died today. Or yesterday maybe, I don't know. I got a telegram from the home: 'Mother deceased. Funeral tomorrow. Faithfully yours.' That doesn't mean anything. Maybe it was yesterday." Putting down the manuscript, he then looked at his fellow editors: "Recommendation one, naturally." According to the house code, this meant that the book ought to be published.[6] The gathered writers agreed that they had just been introduced to a stunning new voice in French literature.

Camus had worked on what he called "the three absurds"—*The Stranger, The Myth of Sisyphus,* and *Caligula*—during his years with *Alger-Républicain,* the Théâtre du Travail, and the Théâtre de l'Equipe. The austerity of the language in these works came, in part, from the discipline he had learned as a director and reporter. Soon after join-ing *Alger-Républicain,* Camus wrote in his notebooks: "The true work of art is one which says least."[7] (Not surprisingly, a draft of the opening paragraph of *The Stranger* appears a few entries later.) The spare prose of his dispatches from Kabylia echoed the telegraphic language—what Roland Barthes famously described as the "zero degree of writing"—of *The Stranger.* Many critics discern in Camus's later work a shift away from the ethical perspective of *The Stranger* to a new focus Camus acquired during the war. They argue that from the place of individual revolt against an absurd world staked out by *The Stranger,* he moves to the high moral ground of collective resistance in *The Plague.* But the high ground was already reached in the earlier novel. *The Stranger* is, indeed, a strange book—stranger than usually thought, for reasons rarely discussed.

○ ○ ○

He came, he saw, he shot an Arab: this not only describes the pivotal moment of *The Stranger,* it serves as an epitaph for its protagonist, Patrice Meursault. He is a young man who grows up poor, raised by a mother with whom he shares few words and fewer expectations, and over whom he does not shed a tear when she dies. Unburdened by memories, Meursault is also untroubled by hopes for the future. Though he is bright, Meursault's straitened financial situation forces him to quit school. He works at an Algiers shipping company; when he is not shuffling papers, he escapes to the sea, seduces the occasional woman, sits on his balcony and, savoring a cigarette, gazes out at an utterly indifferent world. But for the grace of Louis Germain went Camus perhaps, in the guise of Meursault.

Meursault's lot is not unique: many others have lived equally drab lives; many more have known far worse. What makes Meursault's life different is his refusal or inability to hew it into a meaningful narrative. The traditional, comforting formulas we impose on our life stories are absent here. Instead, Meursault's life is one damn thing after another. There is no logic, no hierarchy of importance, and no effort at synthesis. Like the clatter rising from the street below Meursault's terrace, it signifies nothing. When Meursault's boss offers him a promotion and the chance to move to Paris, Meursault turns him down: "I couldn't see any reason to change my life. Looking back on it, I wasn't unhappy."[8] The problem for the rest of us, if not for Meursault, is that he isn't happy either—he simply is.

One day, Meursault goes to the beach with a woman he has recently met, Marie, and a shady individual, Raymond, who had recently befriended him. A pair of Arabs accosts the men, keen on avenging Raymond's rough treatment of one of the men's sisters. A scuffle ensues near a cluster of rocks on the beach; one of the Arabs draws a knife, slightly wounding Raymond. The two groups separate; the bloodshed should have gone no further. Shortly thereafter, however, Meursault returns to the same spot, where he finds the Arab who had knifed Raymond. Blinded by the merciless light, pounded by the intense heat, his entire body coils—as does his finger on the trigger of a gun Raymond had given him to hold. "The trigger gave; I felt the smooth underside of the butt; and there, in that noise, sharp and deafening at the same time, is where it all started."[9]

"It" for Meursault is what was, is, and will be for most of us: life measured by an artificial conception of time. From a kind of time-less existence—he is uncertain about the date of his mother's death, as he is about her age when she died—an inexorable and steady justice overtakes Meursault's life. Until the moment he pulls the trigger, Meursault is as indifferent to the future as he is to the past. He does not puzzle over his life—events, indeed, are not pieces to a puzzle, for there is no puzzle to piece together. Instead, "life" is a word for the waves of physical sensations that wash over him as constantly as the sunlight and sea. Shortly before the murder, Meursault stops "paying attention" to one of his companions be-cause he is "absorbed by the feeling that the sun was doing me a lot of good."[10] This describes the particular moment but also his life until then. In a number of important respects, Meursault becomes for our century what Jean-Jacques Rousseau's "noble savage" was for the eighteenth century: man before the advent of society. Like Rousseau's savage, Meursault also becomes the yardstick by which that same society can be measured and inevitably found wanting.

Once arrested, Meursault realizes he is not on trial for what he has done—killed the Arab—but for what he is: someone who rejects society's norms and language. His lawyer, as Meursault sees it, "didn't understand me, and he was sort of holding it against me."[11] The presiding judge is equally perplexed: Meursault's inability to answer the judge's questions and to believe in God makes his inquisitor shout: "Do you want my life to be meaningless?"[12] Incapable of following the script that shapes their world, Meursault turns into a pariah. This status is reinforced when the jurors learn that Meursault did not cry at his mother's funeral, that he smoked a cigarette and drank coffee while he kept vigil over her body, and that back home in Algiers he took a date to the cinema before the dirt on his mother's coffin had settled. Through his bare and steely prose, Camus's profile of the "stranger" grows darker and more menacing.

Critics have long accused Camus of dehumanizing the Arab population in his novel, giving them neither distinct personalities, individual names, nor, indeed, any recognizably human traits. Instead, they are little more than features of the Algerian landscape, as inscrutable and harsh as the summer sky or desert. As Conor Cruise O'Brien puts it, "the reader does not quite feel that Meursault has killed a man. He has killed an Arab."[13] But is it so simple? Is it instead possible that Meursault himself has been turned into an "Arab"—namely, a character deprived of his humanity? As David Carroll suggests, Meursault is gradually stripped of everything that identifies him as an individual human being.[14] Looked on with growing incomprehension by the state and its institutions, Meursault drifts further away from our world, from the shores of familiarity. When the judge addresses him as "Monsieur Antichrist," it is hardly a joke: Meursault has been expelled from the human race. He has, in fact, become the Other.

o o o

Driven by the desire to cleanse France of its dubious elements, Vichy quickly set about the task of identifying and isolating "others." It pursued many real and imagined enemies, most notably Communists, Socialists, Freemasons, even the *zazous*, young men and women who wore zoot suits and danced to jazz. But the label was most infamously applied to French Jewry: beginning in October 1940, the regime, which had scarcely finished occupying the hotel rooms in Vichy, announced a series of laws that revoked the legal and civil rights of citizens who happened to have at least three Jewish grandparents. Two years later, in the summer of 1942, the regime launched the first of many roundups of French and refugee Jews; in Paris, gendarmes herded more than twelve thousand men, women, and children into a sports stadium. Nearly all of them were eventually deported to Auschwitz. By 1944, the French police had arrested and deported there more than seventy-five thousand Jews, refugees and citizens alike. By war's end, fewer than two thousand were still alive.

Unlike most French citizens in 1940, Camus had few illusions about Pétain's character or the nature of the regime. Far from a shield to protect the nation and all of its citizens, it represented abject surrender to the occupier's demands. In July 1940, he wrote to Francine from France that Pétain offered only "cowardice and senility" to the defeated nation. As for the regime over which the elderly marshal reigned, Camus saw "pro-German policies, a totalitarian-like constitution, an overwhelming fear of an impossible revolution: all of this to soothe an enemy who will crush us nevertheless and to save privileges which will not be threatened....Terrible days are in store for us."[15] Vichy's anti-Semitism reinforced Camus's grim forecast. After the publication in October 1940 of the first anti-Semitic statute, Camus wrote to a Jewish friend, Irène Djian: "All of this is particularly unjust and despicable...but you need to know that those untouched by the law are not indifferent. I vow to hold fast to everything we hold in common. I will never tire of saying this as long as it remains necessary."[16]

Is it possible that Camus made use of Meursault to say "this" earlier than most others in France? Meursault's transformation into the "Other" mirrors in unsettling ways the transformation of the French Jewish community under Vichy. With the Nazi occupation of the southern zone, any remaining pretense of independence for the Vichy regime was demolished, along with what little protection still remained for French Jewry. In the case of refugees, their lot grew even bleaker than before; the citizenship of those whom France had naturalized was revoked; as for those born French, their status meant little to regimes intent on cleansing the world of Jewry. Ultimately, their crime was to have been born Jews rather than non-Jews. The same logic, it has been suggested, drives Meursault's trial. Indeed, unlike French Jewry, he is guilty of a terrible crime: he has killed a man. But as the reader soon understands, Meursault is tried and found guilty not of this particular crime but instead of the "crime" of not being French. In fact, the prosecution insists that Meursault is "not even human—not in legal terms, but more importantly, in moral, religious and metaphysical terms." Perhaps as horrifying as Meursault's crime is the state's reaction: "He is judged not for what he did, but for what he is."[17]

Camus's deepening horror at Vichy's efforts to wrench Jews from society parallels the reader's growing realization that Meursault has also been expelled from our world. Underscoring his personal and moral stake in both contexts, Camus introduces a journalist, nameless like the murdered Arab, into *The Stranger*. On the first day of the trial, Meursault notices him. This particular reporter is younger than his colleagues and, unlike them, looks intently at Meursault. "All I could see in his slightly lopsided face were his two very bright eyes, which were examining me closely without betraying any definable emotion. And I had the odd impression of being watched by myself."[18] When the court sentences Meursault to death, the journalist again appears: this time he turns away, unable to look at Meursault. The shame we feel at a fellow human being's undoing, reflected in the reporter's averted gaze, matches what the young *pied noir* reporter had felt on the prison ship docked at Algiers a few years before.

But in 1942, averting one's gaze or simply "watching oneself" was no longer appropriate. Instead, attending to *others* was now called for. Camus's notebooks reveal that he grew increasingly dissatisfied with the austere conception of the absurd expressed in *The Stranger*. In the silence of Le Panelier, he reminded himself that to revise or reject what one had previously believed was not a weakness. For example, he asked himself, what should we make of the philosopher who announces, "Up to now I was going in the wrong direction. I am going to begin all over"? The public would ridicule him, of course: but what of it? Especially when, as Camus insists, the philosopher would thus be "giving proof that he is worthy of thought."[19] A different order of understanding and ethics was necessary, one that encompassed others rather than isolating the individual subject. Society, not the individual, was now the measure of meaning. As Camus scribbled, the absurd *"teaches* nothing."[20] How are we to act—what are we to do—in a world shorn of God or meaning? The answer, Camus concluded, lay in the solidarity of human beings.

Remarkably, Camus came to this answer at the very moment when the inhabitants of Le Chambon-sur-Lignon, a Protestant village a few kilometers from Le Panelier, were acting on the same insight. The villagers of Le Chambon created a refuge for Jews, in particular children, fleeing the gestapo as well as the Vichy paramilitary forces. By the end of the war, these few hundred Huguenots had saved the lives of several thousand men, women, and children, most of whom had already lost their parents at Auschwitz.[21] Was

Camus aware of these activities? Perhaps. On the one hand, he left no record of such knowledge in his notebooks or in accounts to friends and colleagues; on the other hand, this was precisely the sort of knowledge one would deliberately keep from friends and out of notebooks.

Nevertheless, the simultaneity of Camus's discovery and the activity in Le Chambon is striking. The *pied noir* novelist and the farmers of the Cévennes found common ground in their insistence on the dignity of each and every human being. As André Trocmé, the village minister, told the police officer who demanded to know the whereabouts of the refugee Jews: "We do not know what a Jew is. We know only men."[22] In "Summer in Algiers," an essay published on the eve of the war, Camus declared: "I am learning that there is no superhuman happiness, no eternity outside the curve of the days. These ridiculous and essential assets, these relative truths are the only ones that move me."[23] Even closer to Trocmé's blunt assertion is the observation Camus made in his notebook during the same period: "The misery and greatness of this world: it offers no truths, but only objects for love. Absurdity is king, but love saves us from it."[24]

o o o

The question now became how best to serve this love. The answer for Camus arrived in 1943 when Pascal Pia, the former editor in chief of *Alger-Républicain,* who had assumed the same function at *Combat,* invited Camus to join the paper. Working at first from nearby Lyons, then soon after in Paris, where he moved toward the end of 1943, Camus helped lay out the pages for the paper, while also editing and writing. In early June 1944, when Pia left the paper to take on new responsibilities in the Resistance, Camus replaced him. By then, more than 300,000 copies of a single issue were being printed, reaching a far greater audience than *Alger-Républicain* ever did.

When France was liberated, *Combat* was widely seen as the voice of the Resistance. Yet that voice grew hesitant during the confused and complex period called the *épuration*, or purge. Four years of increasingly brutal occupation had sowed the seeds for revenge. But the nature of the harvest remained unclear. In 1944, the various resistance movements, brought together as the Conseil National de la Résistance (CNR), had vowed punishment for all those who collaborated with the Germans. But the CNR—an uneasy coalition of fractious and mutually suspicious movements—failed to spell out the details.

The devil, it now became clear, was in those details. Had the Provisional Government under Charles de Gaulle applied the criteria for collaboration in a consistent manner, France's industrial, financial, legal, and administrative ranks would have been decimated. This policy would not only have undermined the nation's economic recovery but would also have contradicted the Gaullist myth of France as a nation of resisters. As a result, most professions were largely untouched by the official purge. Ultimately, the courts convicted and imprisoned about 32,000 individuals, most of whom were freed by the early 1950s. Another 7,000 were sentenced to death for treason or collaboration, but in most cases their sentences were commuted.

Those who reaped the nation's collective wrath were the most vulnerable, like the women accused of "horizontal collaboration"— sleeping with the enemy. They were subject to the humiliation of having their heads shaved, then were frequently marched naked or with a swastika sewn on their clothes through a city's central square. Then there were the collaborationist artists, writers, and journalists. These men were targeted for many reasons. First, there was their peculiar place in French history: as far back as Voltaire, the intellectual had widely been seen as the nation's conscience and the defender of justice. Second, unlike the work of bankers or bureaucrats, the intellectual's activities were necessarily public and the paper trail clear and indisputable. But the purge of intellectuals was most severe because intellectuals themselves supported it: "If collaborating intellectuals were important persons who deserved to be judged for their words, then intellectual resisters could make the same claim, both for their role in the war years and for their place in postwar society."[25]

Camus had no doubt about the political and moral tasks the intellectual—more specifically, the journalist—was expected to assume. Just weeks before the liberation of Paris, he aimed a cutting riposte at Marcel Déat. A collaborationist politician and journalist, Déat had declared that under Vichy the métier of journalism had finally become respectable. Indeed it had, Camus replied, thanks to the journalists who risked their lives with the underground papers: it was the independence and dangers of the clandestine life that made journalism honorable.[26] Under Vichy, he declared in another issue, he and his peers "wrote articles knowing that their only remuneration could well be prison or death. Such men know the value of words; they know that words must be chosen carefully."[27]

To be sure, while Camus escaped arrest, several others on the staff of *Combat* were not as fortunate. His colleague Jacqueline Bernard was arrested and deported to Ravensbruck, but returned alive to France. Less fortunate was the paper's printer in Lyons, André Bollier, who committed suicide soon after his arrest by the Germans. One of *Combat*'s founders, Claude Bourdet, survived several concentration camps, while journalist and poet René Leynaud, who served as leader of one of *Combat*'s regional intelligence networks, was captured and executed by the Germans in May 1944.[28]

The impact of Leynaud's death on Camus was particularly great: the two young men had often met in Lyons or Saint-Etienne, discussing the thought of Martin Buber one moment, the sport of boxing the next, as they strolled from one sad and deserted café to the next.[29] Leynaud, a devout Catholic, also helped Camus work through the ethical complexities of resistance. Camus struggled with these same issues in one of his major contributions to the intellectual resistance, a series of letters, three of which were published clandestinely between 1943 and mid-1944. A fourth letter was added to the collection, published after the liberation and titled *Letters to a German Friend*.

Dedicated to the memory of Leynaud, Camus's "letters" were addressed to an imaginary German friend, with whom Camus shares a Nietzschean outlook and nihilist predilections. Given this common starting point, Camus wonders, how can he justify the resistance activities for which Leynaud had given his life? Can one establish a moral case for resistance if, as Nietzscheans, they both believed transcendental meaning to be a dodge and religion a hoax?

Yes, Camus concluded. It required time and thought—indeed, it required the "detour" of war and occupation—but Camus was now certain that justice was on his side. The absence of meaning is not a call to despair or an invitation to leap joyfully into the abyss. Instead, the world's stubborn silence leads us to acknowledge our common predicament and spurs us to rebel against it. In response to both the German nihilist and the Christian believer, Camus still refuses a "greater meaning" to the world. But, he continues, something *in* the world does have meaning: namely, man. We alone, Camus observes, "demand that meaning exist." Our dignity and everyday nobility reside precisely in that insistence. Rather than "mutilating" man, as the Nazis did, we must safeguard the ideal of justice that man alone is capable of conceiving.[30]

In a way, everything and nothing changed between Meursault's imprisonment and that of France. The same pitiless heavens, the same relentless sun span the short and absurd human lives unfolding in both places. As Camus confesses in his last letter, "I know that the sky, which was indifferent to your appalling victories, will be equally indifferent to your just defeat. I expect nothing from it, even today." What has changed, however, is the nature of our response. Rather than act alone, we must act in the company of others. As Camus concludes, the Resistance "will have at least helped save man from the solitude you sought to send him."[31]

As philosophy, *Letters to a German Friend* falls short. The pieces contain a number of dubious or inconsistent claims—Camus's insistence on the necessity of the experience of the Occupation to guarantee the purity of the Resistance, for example, is historically and logically nonsensical. The Resistance was guilty of morally questionable actions—actions occluded or overlooked in the years after liberation. Also, if resisters acted justly only after the "detour" of the Occupation what must we conclude about the prescient and brave few who resisted from the very start? Were they hasty or misguided?

But the reader should not judge the *Letters* in such narrow terms. Rather than a philosophical essay, it is an essay in a broader and different sense: a testing and questioning of propositions that Camus had once held to be true. As with so much else in his intellectual career, Camus carried out this self-questioning in public. And he did so at a time when "hesitation"—the activity that he casts in heroic terms—was a rare and threatened commodity. This became brutally clear during the postwar trial of Robert Brasillach.

o o o

In Paris on the night of January 25, 1945, sleep did not come easily to either Camus or Brasillach. Notorious for his defense of fascism before and during the war, Brasillach had just weeks before been sentenced to death for the crime of treason. In his fiction as well as in editorials for the anti-Semitic newspaper *Je Suis Partout*, Brasillach praised the Nazis and the Italian Fascists as models for a French national revival. After France's defeat in 1940, he became the occupied nation's most eloquent voice on behalf of collaboration with Germany. He also became one of the most feared voices for those groups—republicans, Communists, Socialists, and especially French Jews—threatened by that same policy of collaboration. According to Brasillach's taxonomy of national enemies, Communists and Jews ranked at the very top. In 1941, his column in *Je Suis Partout* asked: "What are we waiting for to shoot the Communist leaders already imprisoned?... Against those who want the death of peace and the death of France, EVERYTHING is legitimate."[32]

Brasillach also aimed this horrifying imperative at French Jewry: just months after the July 1942 roundup, Brasillach wrote that a purified France must "separate from the Jews en bloc and not keep any little ones." As a peculiar sign of independence, he insisted on a specifically French form of fascism—"in the same way that Falangism is Spanish and Fascism is Italian"—yet, toward the end of the war, he reminisced about the Occupation: "It seems to me that I've contracted a liaison with German genius, one that I will never forget. Whether we like it or not, we will have lived together. Frenchmen given to reflection, during these years, will have more or less slept with Germany—not without quarrels—and the memory of it will remain sweet for them."[33] Inconsistent, perhaps; appalling, certainly.

On January 25, Camus received a letter from Marcel Aymé. A writer of great talent and unpredictable political sympathies, Aymé had contributed articles to *Je Suis Partout* during the Occupation. But they were literary, not political—and it was precisely on literary grounds that Aymé felt Brasillach should be saved. The former editor of *Je Suis Partout* was too great a literary talent to be executed for his unfortunate flirtation with fascism. In his letter, Aymé asked Camus to sign a petition addressed to Charles de Gaulle, the head of the Provisional Government, requesting the commutation of Brasillach's sentence.

Aymé was not alone. Weeks before, François Mauriac had already spoken on Brasillach's behalf. In a letter read in court, Mauriac declared that the accused writer had created a literary oeuvre that we "can certainly dislike, but which commands our attention." It would be "a loss for French letters if this brilliant mind were forever extinguished."[34] Mauriac's testimony was powerful for a number of reasons. Not only was he one of France's greatest living authors—a status underscored by his membership in the Académie Française—but he had also been a founding member in 1941 of the Comité National des Ecrivains (CNE), a group of writers committed to the Resistance. Two years later, the underground publishing house Editions de Minuit published Mauriac's *Le Cahier Noir*, a journal in which the novelist, under the pseudonym of Forez, denounced Vichy's policy of collaboration. Justice in France would be reestablished, he wrote in a typical passage, once the country "breaks away from [fascism's] embrace, tears its hands away from her throat and its knee from her chest."[35]

Mauriac's resistance writings required great courage: other writers had been arrested or killed for expressing similar sentiments. Police rifled through Mauriac's apartment, while a gang of fascist thugs threatened Mauriac on a Paris street. *Je Suis Partout*, and Brasillach in particular, added to the atmosphere heavy with menace. Time and again in the pages of his newspaper, Brasillach derided the older writer's bourgeois aesthetic and Catholic faith—criticism easier to ignore than the young critic's taunts that Mauriac was an antifascist and a leader of the "Academy of Dissidence."

Just days passed between the liberation of Paris and Mauriac's warnings against the excesses of the Resistance. Repelled by the explosions of vengeance in the courts and in the streets, Mauriac feared that the newly reborn republic would prove no better than Vichy: "We aspire to be something better than a nation trading off the roles of executioner and victim. At no price must the Fourth Republic wear the Gestapo's boots."[36] The frail novelist held so stubbornly to his call for caution and clemency that he was soon given the moniker "Saint François des Assises," a witty play on the birthplace of the Christian saint Francis of Assisi and on the term for the French criminal courts, *les assises.*

Scornful of Mauriac's Catholic and bourgeois values, the great majority of *résistants* dismissed his calls for mercy. Mauriac was equally skeptical of his critics, especially the Communists, with whom he was in an uneasy alliance. Yet Mauriac's doubts did not at first extend to Camus. The young French Algerian's editorials had won Mauriac's respect in the days following the city's liberation. Yet by autumn, Mauriac's admiration had soured: he found Camus to be no less unbending than others in his calls for rapid and rigorous justice. However, Mauriac should not have been surprised. In March, de Gaulle had refused to pardon Pierre Pucheu, who as minister of interior under Vichy had been responsible for selecting Communist prisoners to be held as hostages, then executed by the Nazis. In an essay in the underground journal *Les Lettres françaises*—to which Mauriac was a contributor—Camus agreed that Pucheu had to die. "Too many men have died whom we loved and respected," he declared, "too many splendors betrayed, too many values humiliated...even for those of us in the midst of this battle who would otherwise be tempted to pardon him."[37]

This marked a dramatic reversal on Camus's part. He had long been a fervent opponent of the death penalty. Though he cited legal, moral, and philosophical reasons for his opposition, Camus's hatred of capital punishment was first and foremost visceral. In *The Stranger,* he introduced for the first time one of the few stories his mother had ever told him about his father. Lucien Camus rose early one morning to attend the public execution of a man who had murdered an entire family. The reason was simple: the elder Camus thought it his duty to witness the event. When he returned to the house, he said nothing. Instead, he went to bed and vomited. In *The Stranger*, Meursault remembers "feeling a little disgusted by him at the time. But now I understood, it was perfectly normal." What "it" is remains vague: Was the son disgusted by the fact that his father went to see the execution? Or was he disgusted by his father's gut response to his experience? It is impossible to say. Still, it is clear that Meursault now understood something he had previously failed to grasp: "How had I not seen that there was nothing more important than an execution, and that when you come right down to it, it was the only thing a man could truly be interested in?"[38] Under the blazing sun of liberated France, Camus was not unlike Meursault standing on the beach in Algiers. Pushed by the overwhelming pressures of justice, Camus condemned a man to death. It was a decision that clashed with all the values he had once held and a decision he would soon regret.

Camus's unusual reasoning reflects his moral uneasiness. Pucheu's greatest crime, the young editorialist argues, was neither his treason nor the deaths for which he was responsible; instead, it was his "lack of imagination"—by which Camus seems to be suggesting his lack of humankind's most fundamental trait, empathy. In his capacity as minister, Pucheu believed that nothing had changed with France's defeat and occupation: he remained a creature of the "abstract and administrative system he had always known." Signing these laws in the comfort of his office, Pucheu failed to see they would be "transformed into dawns of terror for innocent Frenchmen led to their deaths."

Pucheu's particular crime forced Camus to measure fully his own words: "It is in the full light of our imagination that we are learning to accept without flinching... that a man's life can be removed from this world."[39] Camus's expression "lack of imagination" anticipated what Hannah Arendt, more than a decade later, would call the "banality of evil."[40] In his postliberation editorials, Camus focused on this same "banal" flaw. At the end of August, reacting to the torture and murder of thirty-four Frenchmen, he exclaimed: "Who would dare speak here of forgiveness?" But, once again, his outrage focused on the torturer's lack of imagination. After depicting the scene where the bodies were found, Camus concludes: "Two men face to face, one of whom prepares to tear off the fingernails of the other who watches him do it."[41]

For Mauriac, someone who would make such an argument was capable of signing the Brasillach petition. Must we not exercise the full extent of our moral imagination, Mauriac asked, in the cases of treason we now confront? If Mauriac had hoped to persuade his younger colleague, he was disappointed: at the end of October, Camus opened his column in *Combat* bluntly: "We do not agree with M. François Mauriac." Yes, excesses had occurred during the purge, but Camus insisted they did not drown out the call for justice: "It is our conviction that there are times when we must silence our feelings and renounce our peace of mind. Ours is such a time, and its terrible law, with which it is futile to argue, forces us to destroy a living part of this country in order that we may save its very soul."[42]

To Mauriac's ears, Camus's reasoning sounded like that of the Inquisition. Even if one could somehow maintain purity, he thought, that goal itself remained undesirable. The climb toward absolute justice could only lead to a fall into barbarism. At the same time, the Catholic novelist rightly sensed Camus's unanswered need for absolutes. "My young colleague is more religious than I had thought," Mauriac replied two days later. "More than I am, in any case. The inquisitors also burned bodies in order to save souls."[43]

With this exchange of editorials, the united front of the Resistance was revealed to be little more than a facade. But Mauriac and Camus, though from different generations and backgrounds and harboring different beliefs, had more in common with each other than with the rest of the Resistance. Both men were preoccupied with the issue of justice, both were acutely aware of humankind's flaws, both insisted on placing the events of the Liberation against a greater and richer background. The inequitable and capricious character of the purge persuaded Mauriac that France had to adopt a policy of national reconciliation. The time had come, he wrote, for a "return to the politics of Henry IV"—the French king who quelled, if only temporarily, France's wars of religion by imposing the Edict of Nantes. Camus, however, dismissed Mauriac's call for toleration on both religious and pragmatic grounds. Christian mercy, he declared, is irrelevant to those "who know no divine justice, but who nonetheless continue to believe in man and hope to achieve his greatness. For such men the choice is between eternal silence and the pursuit of human justice....We choose human justice with all its terrible imperfections; we can hope to make it better only by holding desperately to our honesty."[44]

Mauriac's debate with Camus echoed earlier religious controversies. During the wars of religion in sixteenth-century France, there were two philosophical camps. There were the *dévôts,* committed to the absolute truth of their religion and utterly opposed to compromise. Then there were the so-called *politiques:* like Henry IV, these Catholics and Protestants (Henry IV moved easily between the two) understood that the alternative to mutual toleration was mutual destruction. In postwar France, Mauriac and Camus took up the roles of *politique* and *dévôt,* respectively. Yet a contemporary of Henry IV would understandably have been confused had he witnessed the debate: here was Mauriac, the devout Catholic, posing as a *politique,* while Camus, the unwavering atheist, espoused the purist's position.

Camus was aware of this odd reversal of roles. In a column published the day after Christmas 1944, he declared that moderation, at least in the present circumstances, was not a virtue. Restraint risks "serving those who want to conserve everything, those who have failed to understand that some things must be changed. Our world does not need tepid souls. It needs burning hearts that know how to put moderation in its proper place." No doubt with his thoughts focused on Mauriac, he added: "The Christians of the first century were not moderates."[45] Though he remained forever alien to Augustine's faith, Camus had the same passion for salvation, if only profane, as that "other North African."

Just weeks later, though, Camus had come to doubt the logic of uncompromising justice. Moderation might lead to the freedom of some of the guilty, but better that than the death of innocents—or, at the very least, those whose guilt was no greater than those who escaped similar punishment. The purge had destroyed the illusions of most idealists: not only were certain professional categories untouched while others bore the brunt of the restored republic, but republican justice itself often seemed to give way to personal vengeance. Shortly after New Year's Day 1945, Camus announced that he had had his fill. In an editorial titled "The Purge Has Gone Awry," he quoted a Catholic commentator who had concluded that justice existed only in hell. The French courts, Camus found, were doing everything possible to prove him true. "News writers and editorialists thus have to choose between writing about absurd condemnations and ridiculous acts of forgiveness. Meanwhile prisoners are dragged out of their cells and shot [by lynch mobs] because they have been pardoned."

At this point, Camus still refused to accept that his initial premise was wrong: if justice had been carried out swiftly and fairly, he insisted, it would have been terrible but essential. It had instead been belated and inconsistent. Too much time had passed, too much damage had been done: "People get used to everything, even shame and stupidity. And where could they ask for more shame and stupidity than from their Ministry of Justice?" Camus had been right to insist on justice half a year ago, but he would be wrong to insist on it now. His column ended with a striking confession: "We now see that M. Mauriac was right: we are going to need charity."[46]

Yet Mauriac was less than charitable in his reply: he disdainfully thanked "our young master" for having spoken from the "heights of the works he has yet to write."[47] Stung, Camus insisted that Mauriac had misrepresented his views: "Each time the purge has been discussed, I have spoken of justice while M. Mauriac has spoken of charity. And the virtue of charity is so unassailable that when I demand justice, I seem to be asking for hate." Though the trials had become squalid affairs, the need for justice remained. But what had been a public issue now became personal: underscoring the false choice Mauriac had imposed on him, Camus then did the very same to his antagonist: "As a man, I can perhaps admire M. Mauriac for knowing how to love traitors; but as a citizen, I deplore it, for this love will turn us into a nation of betrayal and mediocrity." Camus thus returned to the fundamental divide between the two men: religious faith. Yes, Camus allowed, Christianity has a kind of greatness. But it has an even greater irrelevance for "those in this tormented world who believe that Christ may have died to save others, but that he did not die to save us." As a result, "we will forever refuse a divine charity which frustrates the justice of men."[48]

Days after this bitter exchange, Camus took a leave of absence from *Combat*. His sudden prominence as an intellectual, his editorial responsibilities at the paper, his duties at Gallimard—the prestigious publishing house where he had joined Paulhan's cabal of readers—and his weakened lungs in the wet chill of Paris had all weighed greatly on the young provincial. On January 18, Camus addressed a short message to the readers of *Combat*, in which he cited poor health as the reason for his temporary leave. According to one friend, Camus's physical state seemed so grave that he described it as "terminal."[49]

The clash with Mauriac, followed by the Brasillach petition, did little to improve Camus's physical and emotional health. Though he left no record of his reflections, according to Camus's family, he spent the night of January 25 pacing the floor of his studio, wondering how to reply to the request. He perhaps recalled the story of his father's experience of an execution, and perhaps as well, Meursault's reflection that execution is the only thing that can interest us. By the end of his deliberations, Camus returned to his prewar conviction: we must never kill a human being on behalf of an abstract principle. The fog of language and abstractions blinds us to the reality of the men and women and children whom the state condemns to death. As Camus later wrote, his father had "discovered the reality hidden behind our majestic phrases." Instead of recalling the criminal's victims as he witnessed the execution, all he could think of "was this breathing body that had just been thrown across a board in order to chop off its head."[50] Camus fully retreats from the position he had held during the early phase of the purge. His case for Pucheu's execution—the man deserved to die because of his lack of moral imagination—was now applied to the question of Brasillach's petition: it is essential that we, at least, exercise our moral imagination, even, perhaps especially, for a man like Brasillach.

This belief was at the heart of the letter Camus wrote two days later to Jacques Isorni, Brasillach's lawyer, informing him that he had signed the petition because of his opposition to the death penalty. That same day, he wrote a letter to Aymé in which he explained his decision at greater length: "I have always held the death sentence in horror and judged that, at least as an individual,

I couldn't participate in it, even by abstention. That's all. And this is a scruple that I suppose would make Brasillach's friends laugh. It is not for him that I join my signature to yours. It is not for the writer, whom I consider of no significance. Nor for the individual, whom I disdain with all my might. If I had even been tempted to be interested in him, the memory of two or three friends who were mutilated or gunned down by Brasillach's friends while his newspaper encouraged them to do it would have prevented me."[51]

Though he sent his reply to Aymé, Camus must have had Mauriac in mind as well. The same concerns and the same critical jabs from their public exchanges carried over to the letter. But the debate's most important issue—whether the world is ultimately meaningful—received Camus's greatest attention. Not only did he dismiss the notion that the future of French literature rode on Brasillach's pardon, he also rejected the notion that the future of his own soul depended on it. It is precisely because there is no world after this—precisely because, like Brasillach, he is condemned to live in this world—that Camus signed the petition. In his notebook, he raised once again the question that divided him from Mauriac: How can one live without grace? His answer was brutal: "One has to try it and do what Christianity never did: be concerned with the damned."[52] In a world stripped of absolute truths, the most absolute of acts, the killing of a fellow human being, must not be committed in the absence of overwhelming reasons. "We must not condemn others to death because *we* have been given the death sentence."[53] A man of imagination could not say or do otherwise: "The writer condemned to *understanding*," he concluded, "cannot be a killer."[54]

Nor, as it turned out, could such a writer always stop others intent on killing. After reviewing Brasillach's file, including the petition signed by Camus and Mauriac, de Gaulle refused the request for a pardon. On February 6, Brasillach was executed by firing squad. In his memoirs, de Gaulle pauses over this event. His principle in capital cases, he writes, was to commute death sentences if the guilty party had not served the enemy directly. But in Brasillach's case, he continues, "I didn't feel I had the right to pardon. For in literature as in everything, talent confers responsibility."[55]

Camus did not disagree with de Gaulle, but he also dismissed such a justification as irrelevant. Talent certainly confers a degree of responsibility, but our common predicament imposes an even greater form of responsibility: never to lose sight of our common humanity. This marks the true and lasting difference between Camus and de Gaulle—or, for that matter, between Camus and Mauriac. When one of his subordinates suggested at the time of Brasillach's trial that he turn over the power of pardon to one of his ministers, de Gaulle refused: "It is the royal prerogative par excellence, the highest responsibility of a head of state, the only one that he cannot delegate. For that, and for nothing else, do I have to account only to God."[56] Though Mauriac drew a very different conclusion, he shared the otherworldly premise with de Gaulle. For the novelist, God led to clemency, while for the general, God led to severity. But where does this lead a man for whom God does not exist? How can it help a man who, in Camus's phrase, is a "stranger to God"?

∘ ∘ ∘

Most immediately, it led Camus away from political debate and back to writing. In a notebook entry made toward the end of 1946, Camus wrote: "Prepare a book of political texts around Brasillach."[57] Tellingly, the plan was never realized. It is as if Camus understood that the answers would not be found in tracts and treatises but instead in narrative, specifically novels. It is during this period that he was trying to complete the book he started at Le

Panelier: *The Plague*. But shortly before the quarrel with Mauriac, and with himself, over the nature of justice, Camus had already published a defense of novel writing as a moral activity.

"Our greatest moralists are not makers of maxims—they are novelists." In 1944, Camus thus reintroduced the French to the eighteenth-century writer Sébastien-Roch Nicolas Chamfort.[58] It was a small book printed by a small publisher based in Monaco, but the autobiographical element in Camus's introduction is extensive. A commoner from the provinces, Chamfort went to Paris where, by virtue of much talent, ambition, and good looks, he became a fixture in court and society. Once he became a celebrated writer, however, Chamfort maintained a clear and disabused gaze on a world where he always felt like an outsider. Come 1789, he was an ardent supporter of the Revolution: few men were better prepared to embrace the call for liberty. In 1793, when the Reign of Terror was instituted, he became one of the Revolution's most hostile critics: few men were more clear-eyed about the excesses of freedom. Threatened with arrest by the Jacobin authorities, he tried to kill himself: first with a gun (succeeding only in shattering his nose and an eye), next with a knife (cutting his throat, but not deeply enough), then with a letter opener, which he plunged into his chest. The third time was not the charm: he was found still alive in a pool of blood. Chamfort's extraordinary and extraordinarily botched effort left him maimed and weakened until his death in 1794.

Camus seized on the parallels between his own life and Chamfort's. This is clear in his presentation of Chamfort's great literary work, his *Maxims and Thoughts*. There are few things in the world less general or abstract than the human heart, Camus notes. As a result, there is little we learn of true value from the most celebrated maker of maxims, La Rochefoucauld. Camus argues that the taut logic and polished rigor of La Rochefoucauld's phrases disguise the particularities of our lives. One might as well read Euclid for insights into human nature. True moralists do not turn phrases; they turn to look at others and within themselves. They do not codify our behavior but instead describe it. Unlike La Rochefoucauld, Chamfort did not chisel maxims from the recalcitrant stuff of our lives. Instead, like a painter, he worked in sharp strokes and sudden bursts of light. Camus writes that though Chamfort was not thought of as a novelist, his anecdotes and maxims are "hidden novels," a sort of human comedy shaped by a plot and led by a hero. And this is as it should be: "Only the novel is faithful to the specific: it does not offer conclusions about life but instead reveals its unfolding."[59]

For Camus, Chamfort's story is one of loneliness and, ultimately, defeat. To be sure, Chamfort was successful: but "social success only means something in a society one believes in."[60] What is a man of character to do when condemned to live in a world he scorns? Camus's Chamfort, it turns out, offers the same answer as Camus's Sisyphus: he must "take on the demands this world cannot meet. Not in order to be an example to others, but instead by the simple desire for coherence." He died as he lived: equal to himself. "This novel of a superior soul ends in a bloodbath, in the midst of a world turned upside down where dozens of heads were lopped off every day, bouncing into the bottoms of baskets."[61]

For Camus, this violent end furnishes a clearer idea of both Chamfort's life and of morality itself. But it also furnishes a clear idea of Camus's expectations of art. With a consistency as merciless as Chamfort's, some philosophers now claim that philosophy is not well suited for treating questions of ethics and moral responsibility. Through the practice of their craft, novelists lead us to moral insights missed by professional philosophers. Iris Murdoch, who practiced in both fields, argues that novelists alone reveal the evaluative and experiential nature of moral activity. By means of a complex narrative, the evolution of characters, and the development of perspectives, the novel provides an apprenticeship in life. For Murdoch, the sharpening of our imagination and the deepening of our sensitivity to life's intricacies make us better people. Moral philosophy, she writes, "should be inhabited."[62] And literature permits us to relive our lives—to *inhabit* the histories in our wake. Taking her cue from life, the novelist rebuilds the set, recasts the characters, and re-creates life:

> Good art reveals what we are usually too selfish and too timid to recognize, the minute and absolutely random detail of the world, and reveals it together with a sense of unity and form....We are presented with a truthful image of the human condition in a form which can be steadily contemplated; and indeed this is the only context in which many of us are capable of contemplating it at all.[63]

Murdoch's artist works in a world torn from the "permanent background to human activity...whether provided by God, by Reason, by History, or by the self."[64] In this fallen world, literature serves as our map or our moral compass, guarding us from the bogs of fantasy and ideology. For Murdoch, Camus is an exemplary guide: as she said of one of his characters, he is "forever conscious of the possibility of the absurd, but does not relax his grip nevertheless."[65] Grappling with the terrible issues raised by the occupation and liberation of France, Camus for the most part did not relax his grip. He faltered for a moment during the early stages of the purge, but paradoxically did so in the name of moral imagination. But the contradictions of his stance quickly became clear to him—so clear that, by 1945, Camus declared that the "word *purge* is painful enough in itself. That which it describes has become hateful."[66] The power of abstraction had carried away so many others, but Camus, as novelist and moralist, held fast to the particularities of the human situation.

During a lecture to an audience of Catholics at the convent of Latour-Maubourg shortly after the war, Camus looked back on his disagreement with Mauriac. He had been guilty, he recognized, of a lapse of moral attention. The "feverish nature of the time, the memory of two or three assassinated friends," Camus confessed, led to his "pretentious" claims on behalf of justice. But he had never stopped thinking about those events: his dialogue with Mauriac carried over into his fiction. *The Plague* is a continuation of that dialogue by other means. And by dialogue Camus does not mean the exchange of commonplaces and the effort to avoid disagreement. It is, instead, the frank, often brutal and bruising clash of worldviews. As he warned his audience at Latour-Maubourg, "I will not try to modify any of my convictions or any of your convictions so as to obtain a mutually agreeable solution. On the contrary, I am here to tell you that the world needs true dialogue. This has nothing to do with either lies or silence. Dialogue is possible only between those who insist on remaining who they are and on speaking their minds."[67] But remaining who you are does not mean holding fast to illusions or mistakes. And speaking your mind means speaking to errors you have made, no less than to truths you have tested. In his speech, Camus announced that "Monsieur Mauriac was right and I was wrong."[68] For many, this confession reveals great candor and self-discipline; for others, it smacks of grandstanding and theatrical excess. Both sides miss the point, however. Camus's admission is nothing more than an insistence that the dialogue must continue: "I share your horror of evil," as he told his listeners, "but I do not share your hope."

CHAPTER THREE

1952

FRENCH TRAGEDIES

Tragedy is not a solution.

In December 1951, Camus confided to his journal: "I await with patience a catastrophe that is slow in coming."[1] Perhaps he was referring to his physical health: despite a new regimen for his battered lungs, Camus still had difficulty breathing. Or perhaps he meant his writing. His long essay *The Rebel* had been published less than two months before. Many years in the making, the book needed just weeks for its unmaking in the press. While *The Rebel* drew praise as well as criticism, Camus was at times as suspicious of the one as of the other: the conservative *Le Figaro* applauded it, as did the reactionary newspaper *Action Française*. He was also dismayed by criticism from friends. Even Maurice Nadeau, Camus's old colleague at *Combat*, was of two minds. While he thought the book a lucid analysis of their era, Nadeau felt it lacked a clear prescription. Nadeau feared that, at worst, Camus had written a plea on behalf of quietism. He was not alone to wonder if Camus was justifying political conservatism and warning against progressive ideals.[2]

If the book's mixed reception was part of the catastrophe Camus expected, the other part was the silence of *Les Temps Modernes*. Founded by Jean-Paul Sartre shortly after the war, the literary monthly had quickly become the leading voice of the nation's intellectual elite. Its board of editors, including Sartre, Simone de Beauvoir, and Maurice Merleau-Ponty, prided itself on its democratic decision-making. The journal also embodied the newly founded Sartrean imperative of political commitment: the editors cast themselves as advocates for the oppressed workers at home and the colonized peoples abroad. While often critical of the Soviet Union, the journal's great bête noire was the United States. For these intellectuals the two countries pointed to two very different futures: the first, despite its current problems, worked for most of humankind; the second, *because* of its current success, failed most of humankind. For *Les Temps Modernes*, the cultural and political ends of Western liberalism were as toxic as the means, whereas the ends of communism ultimately justified the means, no matter how appalling those means might be. Sartre and his colleagues had set themselves a formidable task: to depict as honestly as possible the horrors of communism, yet frame them so as "to be left with an experience and a project worthy of their dreams and defensible in their own philosophical and ethical language."[3]

In August 1951, the journal had published an excerpt dealing with Nietzsche and nihilism from Camus's still-unpublished book. But more than six months after the publication of *The Rebel*, the journal had not reviewed it. Lack of attention was not the issue— on the contrary, *The Rebel* was the perennial subject at the biweekly meetings of the editorial staff at Sartre's apartment. While bagpipes blared next door—Sartre's neighbors were Breton musicians—the editors drank framboise and smoked pipes and Gauloise cigarettes, the acrid smoke settling over the intellectual scrum as they debated the great issues of the day. At each meeting, Sartre would ask for volunteers to review the book. No one stepped forward. On the one hand, everyone dismissed the book as a superficial and reactionary pastiche of Marxist theory and practice. On the other hand, Sartre, though he shared this opinion, would not allow anyone, including himself, to say so in public. Though relations had cooled between the two writers, Sartre remained attached to the memory of a remarkable friendship. How, Beauvoir wondered, would they "get out of this dilemma"?[4] As tragedy would have it, there was no "getting out" of the situation, a truth the antagonists themselves probably sensed.

o o o

Few individuals were more familiar with tragedy than the mythological Greek hero Orestes. Standing in front of a frenzied mob calling for his death, he recalled that fifteen years before, another murderer, Aegisthus, had stood before them and became king. He had killed Orestes' father Agamemnon, then wed Agamemnon's widow, Clytemnestra, an accomplice to the murder. Yet Aegisthus lacked the courage to proclaim his deed—a cowardice no different from that displayed by those he now ruled. Orestes rebelled against such behavior. "I claim my crime," he shouts, "which is why I make you tremble." Rather than taking the throne, however, he takes the crimes of others on himself, represented by the great swarm of flies plaguing the city ever since the regicide. "Farewell, my fellows: try to live. Everything here is new, everything to be begun. For me, as well, life begins—a strange life." Striding through the stunned crowd, flies in close pursuit, he recites a story: rats had infested another city until a flute player appeared and led them away. "Step aside," he commands. Exit stage left.

On June 3, 1943, eight years before the controversy surrounding *The Rebel*, the House of Atreus had opened for business in

German-occupied Paris. The curtain at the Théâtre de la Cité was raised that day on *The Flies*, Sartre's retelling of the tormented story of Orestes and his family. As in Aeschylus's trilogy *The Oresteia*, Sartre's version of the family was a marvel of dysfunction: murder, matricide, and mayhem mark the descendants of Atreus. Also, as in ancient Greece, the play was performed during the day. Aeschylus exploited the course of the sun: the trilogy begins with literal and metaphorical darkness in occupied Argos; the dawning of Orestes' understanding parallels the sun's rise; and the climax of the final play, *The Eumenides*, unfolds at high noon. Admittedly, Sartre and the director, Charles Dullin, did not have the same motive: power shortages were so common in occupied Paris that they did not want to risk darkness falling at the wrong moment during their production.

But the similarities ended there. In Aeschylus, Orestes flees Argos for Athens, pursued by the Furies, the avenging gods who demand compensation for the murder of his mother, Clytemnestra. A political refugee, Orestes is defended by Apollo in front of a jury of Athenian citizens. After Apollo and the Furies make their arguments, the jury votes: half the jurors condemn Orestes for killing his mother, the other half justify his act. Athena steps in and makes the Furies an offer they cannot refuse: in return for releasing Orestes, Athena will turn them into the Eumenides, or Kindly Ones. They will defend the liberty and independence of Athens, and in return will be worshipped by the citizens of the youthful polis. As the play ends, the Kindly Ones, followed by the audience of Athenian citizens, march solemnly down the aisles and out of the amphitheater. Gods and mortals join hands, democracy and reason triumph, and the demands of justice and mercy dovetail.

A swastika-draped Paris and a divided France were much harsher ground than ancient Athens and a united Greece for such a founding myth. At the end of *The Flies*, Sartre does not bring the characters together, united by a common goal, but leaves them isolated and hostile. The Furies' desire for vengeance is not slaked, the mob's rage is not calmed, and Orestes abandons the city, flies in pursuit. In Aeschylus, Orestes hesitates before he murders his mother; in Sartre, Orestes celebrates the act: violence, it seems, makes the *résistant*.

Violence, however, seemed alien to Sartre, a bookish and un-prepossessing man who, before the curtain rose, stood nervously by the ticket window. One of the spectators, though he had never before met Sartre, recognized him as he entered the foyer. Dapper and tanned, the young man walked up to the young playwright and introduced himself as Albert Camus.[5] The men exchanged little else apart from pleasantries: all in all, a banal first encounter for what would become the most significant friendship in both their lives. The play raised questions that joined the two writers and led to answers that drove them apart nearly a decade later. Come 1952, the public quarrel between Camus and Sartre did not rival the tragic scale of their Greek models, but it revealed that abiding lesson of Aeschylean tragedy: the law demands that we suffer into truth.

o o o

During the war, a number of French writers viewed their predicament through the prism of ancient Greek literature. This was as true for collaborators as for resisters, for reactionaries as for revolutionaries. The ideologue Charles Maurras, convicted of treason in 1945, had long presented France as the inheritor of ancient Greek values—values that happened to exclude from the nation those he called *métèques* (from the Greek "metic," or foreigner), most notoriously the Jews. In the days leading up to his arrest and imprisonment, the virulently anti-Semitic Robert Brasillach was finishing an anthology of Greek poets ranging from Sappho to Theocritus.

The Left was equally under the spell of ancient Greece. In 1943, the same year *The Flies* was panned by Brasillach's *Je Suis Partout* for its moral decadence, Jean Anouilh's adaptation of Sophocles' *Antigone* opened in Paris. Anouilh's presentation of the conflict between Creon, the defender of secular order and political realism, and Antigone, the guardian of eternal laws and ethical idealism, found partisans in both ideological camps. The Resistance embraced Antigone, who defies the demands of the state, while collaborationists cheered Creon, whose responsibility to a battered city obliges him to punish Antigone for her resistance.

Camus had long been interested in the Greeks: in 1937, he staged Aeschylus's *Prometheus Bound* for the Théâtre du Travail. For Camus, meaning, from Aeschylus's merciless perspective and in his enigmatic universe, was "difficult to decipher because it dazzles us."[6] Bound by the gods for all eternity to a rock in hell for having brought fire to mortals, Prometheus does not regret his act. Mocked by Hermes for not having foreseen his punishment, Prometheus, in Camus's play, contradicts him: "I *did* see it."[7] As his *Letters to a German Friend* already announced, the true rebel acts in full knowledge that there will be no ultimate vindication or justification. The Promethean individual, Camus declared, knows "all too well that blind justice does not exist, that history has no eyes, and that we must therefore reject its justice in order to replace it as much as possible with the justice conceived by the mind."[8] Camus clung to this understanding of the Promethean myth for the rest of his life.

o o o

During the performance in 1943 of Sartre's *The Flies*, Camus must have been struck by Orestes' parting story of a vermin-besieged city. He, too, was working on a story about plague, with a cast of characters that included thousands of rats. But as he labored over the early drafts, Camus was not sure what kind of story it would be. It was, he told Jean Grenier, "a sort of novel." A sort of novel, moreover, in search of a title: at various moments, Camus plumped for *The Prisoners, The Exiles,* and *The Separated.* Eventually he chose the name under which the novel was published in 1947, two short years after France's liberation: *The Plague.* Yet, even on the eve of its publication, Camus was mined by doubts: "In my whole life, never such a feeling of failure. I am not even sure of reaching the end. At certain moments, however..."[9]

Camus's fears were unfounded: *The Plague* immediately became a best-seller translated into dozens of languages. The novel follows a group of men who share nothing except their location—the Algerian city of Oran—when an outbreak of bubonic plague occurs. The city is placed under quarantine and the men join forces to resist the plague's onslaught. Though the impact of their "resistance" seems trivial—the number of plague victims mounts inexorably—its moral significance is great: the act of rebellion, the insistence on lucidity and understanding, defines a new form of heroism. When the plague eventually recedes, it leaves behind both the wreckage of human lives and a record of human dignity and courage.

Most of the novel's characters are ne'er-do-wells whose social marginality reflects ethical centeredness. There is Rambert, a journalist who does not write and a thinker who dislikes ideas; Joseph Grand, a petty bureaucrat who spends his life endlessly rewriting the first line to an otherwise unwritten novel; Tarrou, a mysterious figure whose private journal becomes the basis for a public history; Father Paneloux, a priest whose faith proves too austere for his parishioners and perhaps for himself; and Bernard Rieux, a doctor who battles the plague with the knowledge that his efforts are futile.

Early in the novel, Rambert visits Rieux: sent to Algeria by his newspaper, the reporter suddenly finds himself separated from his girlfriend when Oran is quarantined. An enraged, uncomprehending Rambert tells Rieux that he does not belong in Oran: his situation is too absurd for words. A sympathetic Rieux agrees: "Oh, I know it's an absurd situation, but we're all involved in it, and we've got to accept it as it is." When Rambert persists—"I don't belong here"—Rieux replies: "Unfortunately, from now on you'll belong here, like everybody else." Rambert nevertheless makes plans to escape the city. The planning turns out to be more complex than anticipated; while waiting for his opportunity, Rambert joins Rieux and the others on the sanitation teams created to keep the plague at bay. When the chance to escape finally presents itself, Rambert has changed his mind. He tells Rieux he cannot leave Oran "now that I have seen what I have seen."[10]

The other characters also embody the ethics of attention. The narrator, Rieux, declares that his approach is simple: he must gather all relevant evidence. The most valuable, he announces, "is what he saw himself," followed by other eyewitness accounts. As the number of deaths rises in Oran, Rieux tells others what he sees— namely, growing signs of plague—while his colleagues refuse to see these same signs. Though at times he desperately wants to close his eyes to events, he reminds himself that he "must fix his mind...on observed facts." An empiricist, Rieux insists that a life well lived is "a matter of lucidly recognizing what had to be recognized."[11]

But seeing is not always believing, just as believing often has little to do with seeing. Sight demands not just eyes but imagination: without this faculty, we cannot accept and act on what we see. When Rieux confronts the city's prefect with the latest mortality statistics, the official admits they are "perturbing." Rieux blurts out: "They're more than perturbing; they're conclusive." Yet the prefect cannot see what Rieux has placed under his eyes, promising only that he will "ask the government for orders." Echoing Camus's criticism of Pierre Pucheu, Rieux can no longer contain himself: "Orders! When what's needed is imagination."[12] A special kind of sight is called for: one in which we describe others faithfully. This kind of attention necessarily entails that we treat them with consideration.

Even more so than Rieux, Tarrou lives according to this severe imperative. He and Rieux form not just the city's sanitation teams but a friendship as well. One night, after they have completed their rounds, they find themselves sitting alone on a terrace. Despite this perspective, one that overlooks the city, their eyes can see very little: the absence of lighting in the quarantined city leaves the harbor and cliffs in darkness. Only the stars pierce a soupy grayness so thick that Rieux sees little else than Tarrou's stout profile in the chair beside him.

But we learn that there are other and deeper kinds of sight. Agreeing to "take an hour off for friendship," Tarrou tells Rieux about his past. His father was a state prosecutor, a man Tarrou admired during his childhood. One day, Tarrou went to court to watch his father argue a capital crime case. It was an epiphany, but one rooted in this world. Just like Camus's father at the public execution, or Camus himself aboard the prison ship in Algiers or in his Paris apartment agonizing over Brasillach's pardon, the young Tarrou could not see the abstract monster his father was busy portraying but only a man of flesh and blood sitting in the dock. He describes the prisoner to Rieux in great detail, noting that his tie was askew and that he bit the fingers of only his right hand. Then he breaks off: "I needn't go on, need I? You've understood—he was a living human being." Yet his father, a kind and easygoing man, was transformed by the court's traditional red gown he had donned. He spewed out "long, turgid phrases like an endless stream of snakes. I realized he was clamoring for the prisoner's death. . . . 'He must pay the supreme penalty.'" Stunned by the clash between this human being gnawing at his nails and his father's flow of abstract phrases, Tarrou was changed forever. Unable to face his father again, he fled his home for a life of exile. Each of us has the plague, Tarrou tells Rieux, and each of us "must keep endless watch on ourselves lest in a careless moment we breathe in somebody's face and fasten the infection on him." The good man, he continues, "is the man who has the fewest lapses of attention. And it needs tremendous will-power, a never ending tension of the mind, to avoid such lapses." Ultimately, it comes down to seeing and speaking clearly. "All of our troubles," Tarrou concludes, "spring from our failure to use plain, clear-cut language."[13]

For Rieux as for Tarrou, plain speaking is more than just an issue of public policy or scientific study; it is a question of ethical rigor. But Camus knew that this claim is as slippery as it is compelling. On the one hand, he has Rieux assert that, in his written account of the plague, "so as not to play false to the facts, and, still more, so as not to play false to himself, [he] has aimed at objectivity. He has made hardly any changes for the sake of artistic effect."[14] On the other hand, as Camus well knew, you cannot put pen to paper without committing an "artistic effect." This is true for the simplest of texts; how much truer it is for a masterwork such as *The Plague*.

Rieux nevertheless presents his book as a "chronicle" of the plague, suggesting it is more objective than even historical writing. Yet it is oddly unlike a chronicle: it does not even provide precise dates. Moreover, chronicles simply string together events with no concern for plot or meaning—the very last thing Camus wished to write or that we might wish to read. Instead, the narrator's insistence on objectivity reflects less a method than a style, one that points to the writer's relationship not to his material but with his reader.

Here and elsewhere, Camus took a page not from the Greek tragedians or philosophers but from the historian Thucydides. Commentators have long recognized Camus's debt to the ancient historian's description of the plague that swept through Athens shortly after the beginning of the Peloponnesian War in 431 BC. The parallels are many and striking: the swings between hope and despair in Athens, the gradual collapse of traditions and institutions, the festering of superstition and resentment, even the author's claims of objectivity. In all these respects, Camus closely follows Thucydides.[15]

It is telling that just months after France's defeat, Camus committed himself to a course of study: "The Greeks. History—Literature—Art—Philosophy."[16] These various genres, while they differed in form, offered the same urgent wisdom. Camus made this clear when he created a fictional character, Stephan, in early sketches for *The Plague*. Stephan is a classics teacher trapped in an unnamed, plague-ridden city. "He realizes," Camus observed, "that he had not understood Thucydides and Lucretius until then."[17]

Until 1940, neither had Camus. Only now did he see that he and Thucydides had many things in common, beginning with the experiences of exile and defeat. Thucydides started to write his history after being expelled from his native city of Athens (his fellow citizens were unfairly angry over Thucydides' command of a failed naval battle). As for Camus, he undertook *The Plague* only after the authorities in Algiers closed his newspaper, forcing him to move to France for employment. In both cases, exile provided physical and emotional distance to reflect on events.

More intriguing is the common claim to objectivity of Thucydides and Camus. No doubt Camus was attracted to the traditional understanding of objectivity as an ideal. Shortly after the war, he told a friend: "One thing seems to me greater than justice: if not truth itself, at least the *effort* toward truthfulness."[18] But Camus also used objectivity as a narrative technique—the rhetoric of antirhetoric. If objectivity is a strategy, not just a goal, Camus could find no better model than Thucydides. Through the simple juxtaposition of events, Thucydides forces us to consider what we otherwise might have overlooked. Early in his account, he re-creates Pericles' funeral oration, in which the Athenian leader praises the power of human reason to foresee all eventualities. An outbreak of plague immediately follows—an unforeseen disaster, Thucydides notes, that claimed Pericles as one of its victims. By combining the events, he makes clear what pages of emotive prose never could: the hubris of Pericles' claims on behalf of reason. The case against hubris also arises for Rieux's opponent, Dr. Richard. After long denying the plague's reality, Richard finally and grudgingly acknowledges it. He nevertheless predicts its demise based on statistical trends. Hours before a meeting with city officials where he plans to deliver his optimistic assessment, however, he too is "carried off by the plague."[19]

Equally important, both narratives remind us of the limits of narrative. Before he launches into his account of the plague, Thucydides hesitates: "Words indeed fail when one tries to give a general picture of this disease."[20] Rieux is equally diffident: like his Greek predecessor, he dislikes the sort of writing that sways emotions but distorts the truth. Instead, he will use "conventional language," though it was "incapable of describing" the experience of the plague.[21] Yet neither Thucydides nor Camus was satisfied with this initial paradox: both of them double the knot. Confronting an angry city after the plague strikes, Pericles defends himself: he had "at least as much ability as anyone else to see what ought to be done and to explain what he sees. A man who has the knowledge but lacks the power clearly to express it is no better off than if he never had any ideas at all."[22] Clarity and transparency are equally indispensable to history writing: shunning literary flourishes, Thucydides wants only that "these words of mine be judged useful by those who want to understand clearly the events which happened in the past."[23] Similarly, Tarrou insists upon "plain, clear-cut language"; Grand believes "in calling things by their name"; and Rieux uses only "impartial" and "restrained" language to convey the events that have befallen Oran.

Yet this insistence on light in turn dims meanings already obscure. Two millennia after he wrote, Thucydides remains inscrutable *because*, not despite, the forcefulness of his language. The *History of the Peloponnesian War*, which, Thucydides declares, "used only the plainest evidence and...reached conclusions which are reasonably accurate," has divided readers ever since: we still argue over the character of those "reasonably accurate conclusions."[24] His use of sources, contradictory assertions, and refusal to take sides all make for a story whose words are clear but whose meaning is opaque.

So, too, with Camus: all his characters insist on simple language, yet all are condemned to degrees of silence. Grand spends his life rewriting the first line of his novel; Rambert quits his job as a reporter; Tarrou confides only in his private journal; and Rieux is unable to speak truth to bureaucratic power. Accuracy and clarity are paramount concerns, but at the end of both Thucydides' and Camus's works these values appear useless. For Thucydides, history "does not teach us how to control human events, nor enable us to cure plagues or prevent potential tyrannies, but it reminds us how easily men move from the illusion of control over events to being controlled by them."[25] This resembles Rieux's final words: "The plague bacillus never dies or disappears for good;...it can lie dormant for years and years...and...perhaps the day would come when, for the bane and the enlightening of men, it would rouse up its rats again and send them forth to die in a happy city."[26]

Why write, then? Both authors offer the same grim answer. Thucydides asserts his work would be "useful to those who want to understand clearly the events which happened in the past and which (human nature being what it is) will, at some time or other and in much the same ways, be repeated in the future."[27] As for Rieux, he writes to offer a record "of what had to be done, and what assuredly would have to be done again."[28] The implications are tragic: both men seem to ask us to understand a process we cannot change. This certainly seems to be Tarrou's position. When Rieux asks him why he joined the sanitation squad, Tarrou replies: "Comprehension."[29] Of course, Tarrou, Rieux, and the others also act as if they are capable of more than comprehension or diagnosis: they act in the belief they can influence events for the better. Rieux tells Tarrou it is all quite simple: "There are sick people and they need curing."[30] Yet when Tarrou replies that these "victories will never be lasting," Rieux responds: "Yes, I know that. But it's no reason for giving up the struggle."[31]

This is not simple bravado. While the "struggle" is unending, it does not preclude choice. Rather, it makes choice more important: for Rieux no less than for Thucydides, we are fully human only when we act freely. But freedom, in turn, imposes duties—or, in Camus's phrase, "exigencies." As he had already argued in *Letters to a German Friend*, the recognition of the world's absurdity is not license to add to it. Instead, recognition must lead to resistance. But now, with Thucydides at his side, Camus tries to explain why this is so. Along with the ancient Greek historian, Camus asserts that when we act, we must do so fully aware of our limitations: we must act with just measure, basing our actions on concrete and immediate goods instead of abstract and distant ends.

For Rieux, "the most incorrigible vice [is] that of an ignorance that fancies it knows everything." The conviction that one is right, Rieux continues, has disastrous consequences: it "claims for itself the right to kill."[32] It so happens that the Athenians claimed this right, leading to their downfall. In book 5 of his *History*, Thucydides devotes a great deal of space to what seems like a minor event. In 416 BC, an Athenian force besieged Melos, a small island trying to remain neutral in the war between Athens and Sparta. The Athenian envoys told the Melians that neutrality was not an option: you were either with or against Athens. When the Melians protested the injustice of the ultimatum, the Athenians cut them off: "The standard of justice," they proclaimed, "depends on the equality of power to compel and...in fact the strong do what they have the power to do and the weak accept what they have to accept."[33] The Athenians also dismissed the Melian warning that either the gods or the Spartans might come to their rescue. Hope, the Athenians observed, is an expensive commodity. Still, the Melians refused to surrender, leaving the bemused Athenians to observe: "You seem to us quite unique in your ability to consider the future as something more certain than what is before your eyes, and to see uncertainties as realities, simply because you would like them to be so."[34] The siege began, Athens defeated Melos and, as Thucydides concludes, the victors killed all the men and enslaved the women and children.

Following the "Melian Dialogue," Thucydides immediately takes up Athen's fatal decision to invade Sicily—a decision based on the same illusions harbored by the Melians. They confused desire with reality, ignorance with confidence, in attacking an island whose strength and will to resist they had greatly underestimated. Here as elsewhere, Thucydides is "objective": he does not comment on the events he reports. But the order in which he gives the events, rapidly taking the reader from Melos to Sicily, makes all commentary superfluous. Blinded by confidence, Athens took one step too many: its fall would be as great as its hubris.

While Camus never cited this or related passages from *The History of the Peloponnesian War*, we know he read Thucydides, and his writings give every impression that he was familiar with the story.

Camus certainly had time enough in Le Panelier to read the work; and like Thucydides, he had "the leisure to observe affairs more closely." Both men were removed from the immediate pressures that create "unfounded hopes and gratuitous fears."[35] Their experiences of exile ultimately led them both to emphasize the importance of balance and moderation in politics. In an editorial published the same year as *The Plague,* Camus declared that democracy was an exercise in humility. "When parties and peoples are so convinced by their own arguments that they are willing to resort to violence to silence those who disagree with them, democracy no longer exists. Modesty is thus salutary in republics at all times."[36]

This is a thoroughly Periclean sentiment: though the Athenian leader ultimately fell to hubris, for most of his life he embodied the principle of moderation. In his funeral oration, he reminded Athenians that their city was open and law-abiding, committed to balance and dialogue: it was a lesson for all Greece. No less telling, Pericles recalled that in Athens citizens did not "say that a man who takes no interest in politics is a man who minds his own business; we say that he has no business here at all."[37] Similarly, Rieux, Tarrou, and Rambert all declare, at various moments, that the "plague was everybody's business."[38] The difficulty, of course, whether in ancient Athens, fictitious Oran, or postwar France, was to persuade the individual citizen to accept these constraints on their private lives and activities.

o o o

Sartre admired *The Plague.* In 1945, he told an audience in New York that the novel, which he had read in manuscript, embodied the new spirit of resistance and engagement in French letters. And Camus himself, Sartre added, heralded a new kind of artist, committed to bettering society, as well as a new kind of literature—one "without illusions, but full of confidence in the grandeur of humanity; hard but without useless violence, passionate yet restrained." This young writer's courage in dark times and his obstinate belief in the possibilities of humankind offered hope to a generation formed in the crucible of war, occupation, and liberation: "The constant pressure of death, the perpetual threat of torture, made such writers as Camus measure the powers and the limits of man."[39]

By then, the two men had become close friends: Camus had in fact asked Sartre to go to New York as *Combat*'s special envoy. The relationship formed quickly in the tumult of the events of 1944, when Camus brought Sartre into the fold of *Combat*, tasking him with writing a series of articles on the city's liberation. On August 21, while the retreating German forces and the French Resistance were still exchanging gunfire in Paris, Sartre and Beauvoir went to the newspaper's office to deliver his copy. The scene they found there was electrifying: the building was a hive of excitement and fear, with Camus and his colleagues "working with guns at the ready." The doors were locked shut and the staff worried that "at any moment German soldiers could come and it would have been a bad mess."[40]

Under the headline "A Stroller in Paris Unbound!" Sartre's name was the first byline to appear in the newly public newspaper. Yet Sartre's byline was sheer fiction: Beauvoir, in fact, wrote the eyewitness reports. As she confessed late in life, Sartre was himself "too busy" to do so.[41] And in a separate incident, Sartre appeared too tired to take care of Resistance business. During a meeting, he was assigned the task of protecting the vacated Comédie Française in the confusion of half-liberated, half-occupied Paris. Sartre accepted the mission and made his way across the alternately chaotic and empty city to the venerable theater. Once he reached the building, however, he promptly fell asleep in one of the orchestra seats. When Camus found his friend napping, he burst out laughing: "You've placed your seat in the direction of history!"[42] It seemed, as Camus's lighthearted jest suggested, that Sartre was doomed to be forever a spectator, not a participant. But Camus's friendly joke would subsequently take on a far darker hue.

By 1945, Camus's and Sartre's reputations in France and abroad had grown in tandem. The French and foreign press portrayed the two friends as a kind of philosophical tag team, advocates of a new school of thought, existentialism, and practitioners of the new vocation of political engagement. Yet almost nothing could be further from the truth. In 1945, just days after Sartre's celebrated lecture in Paris, "Existentialism Is a Humanism," which launched the movement as France's most prestigious cultural export, Camus gave an interview to a French magazine. When the interviewer referred to the two friends as "existentialists," Camus took issue not with his friendship with Sartre but with the label "existentialist." He and Sartre, Camus joked, had considered "publishing a short statement in which the undersigned declare they have nothing in common with each other."[43]

Camus's tongue was only partly in cheek. Even as the public imagination drew the two men together, their private reflections were pulling them apart. At the very moment Camus was turning away from political engagement and had deepening doubts about the legitimacy of violence for any political end, Sartre was turning toward engagement and increasingly certain of the need for violence to achieve political goals. The movement by each man toward the position the other had previously held was not coincidental, particularly in Sartre's case. Spending the war years as an observer—as a "writer who resisted, not a resister who wrote"—Sartre was overwhelmed by the dashing action figure cut by Camus. Ronald Aronson suggests that Sartre "seemed to assimilate Camus to himself" in his newfound emphasis on engagement: "This young man was already the person Sartre was trying

to become."[44] Several years later, while sifting through the wreckage of their quarrel, Sartre recalled that his former friend lived this
era "more deeply and fully than many of us (myself included)." He
was, Sartre declared, "the admirable conjunction of a person, an
action, and a work."[45] Camus's most remarkable literary creation,
in the end, was not Meursault or Rieux but Jean-Paul Sartre in his
postwar reincarnation as the point man for *littérature engagée.*

Yet did Sartre fully understand how early Camus had distanced
himself from existentialism? Five years before they met, the young
French Algerian writer had already encountered Sartre through
the medium of his first novel, *Nausea.* In a review of the book for
Alger-Républicain, Camus expressed his misgivings. He began with
an axiom: "A novel is nothing more than philosophy expressed
through images." The balance between the two elements is critical:
allow the philosophical ideas to overwhelm the characters and action and the novel becomes lifeless. Camus praised Sartre's "vigor
and confidence" in depicting the collapse of the stage set on which
we live our lives, forcing us to confront our absurd condition. But,
Camus continued, Sartre failed to mesh the narrative and philosophical elements, a gap that hindered the reader from throwing
himself fully into the work. More important, Camus worried over
the abuse of the absurd: "A certain kind of literature makes the
mistake of believing life is tragic because it is miserable." Nothing
could be further from the truth: "Life is tragic precisely because it
is overwhelming and magnificent." It is for this reason, Camus concluded, that the "affirmation of life's absurdity cannot be an end,
but only a beginning."[46]

During the war, Camus grew more convinced than ever that existentialism was a diagnosis mistaken by many for a cure. By itself, it
was, quite simply, "zero point," a datum of existence that "teaches
nothing."[47] The experience of liberation only confirmed this belief:
the existentialist was right to affirm the existence of the absurd but

wrong to propose that we remain there. "Accepting the absurdity of everything around us is one step, a necessary experience," he insisted, but "it should not become a dead end."[48] Just as recognizing a physical illness leads to the search for a cure, recognizing the absurdity of our lives leads to revolt. And the idea of revolt, Camus concluded, "could help us to discover ideas capable of restoring a relative meaning to existence."[49]

o o o

Camus's idea of revolt proved too frail to weather the cold war, which by then had settled over Europe and much of the world. The Soviet Union had recently tested its first atomic bomb, had sponsored the North Korean invasion of South Korea, and had launched a series of show trials in its Eastern European client states. In France, the Communist Party, loyal to Moscow, was the dominant opposition party, claiming the allegiance of the working class and intellectuals. The prophecy made in 1950 by the prominent Communist philosopher Roger Garaudy seemed utterly reasonable to friends and foes alike: "Without any doubt, the twentieth century will go down in history as the century of the victory of Communism."[50] Garaudy's counterpart, the political scientist Raymond Aron, ridiculed such predictions. Still, he allowed that every action in the West "presupposes and involves the adoption of an attitude with regard to the Soviet enterprise."[51]

The "Soviet enterprise" seemed on the verge of establishing a franchise in France. At the very moment U.S. and Chinese forces were about to collide on the Korean peninsula, panic set in around Paris: rumors flared that France was about to be invaded by the Soviet Union. Bumping into Sartre and Beauvoir at a café, Camus asked about their plans should the Russians attack. Before they could reply, he quickly added: "You mustn't stay!" An argument quickly erupted: Camus insisted on the need to resist the Soviet invasion, while Sartre answered that the Soviet Union remained the best hope for French workers. Nonsense, Camus replied angrily: these same French workers had never protested the existence of Soviet labor camps. Sartre would not budge: French workers, he said, already had "troubles enough without worrying about what's going on in Siberia." Camus persisted: "If you stay it won't only be your life they'll take, but your honor as well."[52]

Yet for many Parisians, it seemed, the fear of seeing a red flag flying over city hall was no greater than seeing a "Buvez Coca-Cola" sign blinking above Notre Dame. While the Red Army seemed poised to invade France, the United States had already launched a more subtle kind of invasion, one whose weapons were cultural and commercial exports. These fears came to a head with the battle over Coca-Colonization, fought at the same time as the war engulfing the Korean peninsula. Many on the Right and Left, Gaullists *and* Communists, saw the Coca-Cola Company's efforts in the early 1950s to open bottling plants in France as the beginning of the end of French culture. Doomsayers across the ideological spectrum predicted catastrophe: the eclipse of the wine industry, youth's addiction to the drink's mysterious ingredients, the collapse of social traditions, and the extinction of *la vie douce.* Even the usually sober *Le Monde* declared in 1950, "Coca-Cola is the Danzig of European culture."[53] Allow the Americans this bridgehead, in short, and they would go on to colonize the rest of the Old World.

But the fear went well beyond Coke. As blunt as always, Beauvoir expressed this widespread anxiety. Already disenchanted with the "arrogant condescension" and social conformism she encountered during her visit to the United States a few years before, her attitude toward the U.S. presence in France had darkened. She had come to see the U.S. soldiers in France as no better than the Germans they had forced out: "What their uniforms meant to us now was our dependence and a mortal threat." When she confided to Camus her conviction that France suffered under a new kind of occupation, he was jolted: "Really?" After a short pause, he continued: "Wait a while. You'll see a real Occupation soon—a different sort altogether."[54]

Could a third way be found? In the late 1940s, a small group of non-Communist intellectuals tried to blaze such a path, creating the Rassemblement Démocratique Révolutionnaire (RDR). Sartre and Camus joined the movement, attracted to its effort to tack between Soviet communism and American capitalism. For Camus, at least, the RDR was poised to challenge all extremisms. Speaking at an RDR convention, Camus affirmed that it was better "to be wrong and to have killed no one than to be right and to have contributed to the digging of mass graves."[55] Such prudential declarations failed to stir a mass movement, however. The RDR died an early death, incapable of taking root in the polarized soil of postwar France.

By then, Camus had already left a foundering *Combat*, no less a victim of the times. Like the RDR, the newspaper was an equal opportunity skeptic: it distrusted capitalism as much as communism, the Gaullist RPF as much as the PCF. Proud of its internal debates, the newspaper carried not just Sartre's highly critical dispatches from the United States but pro-American assessments by Raymond Aron. *Combat* was fiercely independent, refusing financial support from political parties and wealthy individuals, but it was penniless. During a printers' strike in early 1947, the paper bled the last of its financial reserves. Camus tried to mask the dire situation. Once the strike had ended, he wrote: "Poor but free before the strike, *Combat* is back, poorer than ever but still free and determined to stay that way."[56] Yet the editorial board's deepening ideological conflicts—some members, like Aron and Albert Ollivier were moving toward the Gaullists, while others looked to the PCF—combined with the paper's financial hemorrhage, led Camus to resign just a few months later. His parting words were grim: "The conditions under which daily newspapers operate have evolved to the point where only large circulation papers can break even. I leave it to readers to ponder what this law of economics portends for freedom of thought."[57]

These same ideological pressures wrenched at Camus and Sartre. It may well be that Sartre's failure to join the Resistance during the war, coupled with the postwar failure of the RDR, made him more determined than ever to plunge into politics. He was already warming up for his leap in *The Flies*. When Orestes murders Aegisthus and Clytemnestra, then quits the city he has just liberated, many in the audience heard the call for violent rebellion against Vichy and Germany. Yet violence was more than a means to liberate France. Sartre has Orestes embrace violence not just as a political necessity but as an ethical imperative as well: only when he kills Aegisthus and Clytemnestra does he become fully himself.[58]

Violence was not committed merely for the sake of self-actualization; it was also the sole means to create a classless and just society. As Sartre's friend and mentor Maurice Merleau-Ponty had just argued in his book *Humanism and Terror*, we do not have a choice between violence and nonviolence. Rather, we have to choose between different kinds of violence. Either we accept the brutal exploitation of workers and colonized peoples under liberalism, Merleau-Ponty states, whose sole end is the continued suppression of entire social classes and continents, or we make the violence of communism our own: there, at least, violence is employed to achieve a future where violence will no longer exist and where all human beings will be free and equal. As Merleau-Ponty argues, "Violence is the common origin of all regimes. Life, discussion, and political choice occur only against a background of violence. What we have to discuss is not violence, but its sense or its future."[59]

The one party in France geared for this battle, promising a better world of "singing tomorrows," was the PCF. Sartre was not blind to Stalin's crimes—to the PCF's great displeasure, he had denounced the existence of the labor camps—but by the early 1950s he had rallied to the Soviet Union as the great remaining hope of the working class. For any committed humanist, Sartre believed, communism was the only game in town. It may well have created a hell on earth in Russia, but it was through this hell that humanity had to pass in order to achieve a better tomorrow. Speaking for Sartre, Beauvoir declared that while far from the "dream of a socialism without defect, Russian socialism had the immense advantage of existing."[60]

Camus despised this logic. The compromises he had made with communism during the war now left him shaken. A chance meeting on a Paris street between Camus and a fellow member of the Resistance reflected the bleak trajectory of politics from the Occupation to the cold war. When the friend told him he had joined the PCF, Camus blurted out: "Then you'll be a murderer." The friend replied that the war had already made him a murderer. Camus answered that the war had done so to him as well: "But I don't want to be any more." As they parted, Camus told him: "This is the real problem: whatever happens, I shall always defend you against the firing squad. But you will be obliged to approve my being shot. Think about that." The friend promised he would.[61]

But at this point it was not clear, at least to Camus, if the friend could honor his promise. Vast and opposing forces had caught the world in a great vise; individual choices seemed limited and bleak. Camus feared Europeans faced a choice between the divine and the "divinization of history"—namely, Marxism's "scientific" affirmation that the logic of history led inevitably to a classless society. "What to do between the two?" he wondered. "Something in me tells me, convinces me that I cannot detach myself from my era without cowardice, without accepting slavery, without denying my mother and my truth....Not a Christian, I must go on to the end. But going on to the end means choosing history absolutely, and with it the murder of man if the murder of man is necessary to history. Otherwise, I am but a witness."[62]

Camus decided that provisional claims and clear speaking are our only alternatives. He made Rieux's ethics his own: he would call things by their name. Like Rieux, Camus rejected abstraction. Both men insisted on describing the world as it was, whether by identifying the buboes erupting on a patient's body or the linguistic subterfuges and cognitive strategies we use to accept our lot. Rieux was scandalized by the deaths of his patients when he first began his practice: "I was outraged by the whole scheme of things," he tells Tarrou. Though the outrage slowly faded over time, it never disappeared: "I've never managed to get used to seeing people die. That's all I know."[63] As he shouts at Paneloux, who tried to justify God's ways following a child's death: "Until my dying day I shall refuse to love a scheme of things in which children are put to torture."[64]

Rieux's confrontation with Paneloux echoes a row between Camus and Merleau-Ponty. During a party hosted by the writer and musician Boris Vian, the guests, including Sartre, Beauvoir, and Merleau-Ponty, had been drinking and debating for several hours when Camus arrived late in the evening. As American jazz blasted over Vian's phonograph, Camus noticed Merleau-Ponty and walked right up to him. Without a pause, he attacked the philosopher for his claim that violence was inherent to politics and, as a result, the violence of communism was preferable to capitalism, for it at least promised a better future. As Merleau-Ponty tried to reply, Sartre jumped into the fray, taking Merleau-Ponty's side. Shocked by his friend's attempt to defend the indefensible, Camus stalked out of the apartment, slamming the door behind him. Sartre ran after him but could not cajole him to return to the party. Six months passed before the two friends spoke again to each other.[65] Camus had no regrets: "Today things are clear and what belongs to the concentration camp, even socialism, must be called a concentration camp. In a sense, I shall never again be polite."[66]

o o o

The Rebel is an essay on the necessity of being impolite. Published in 1951, the book surveyed a modern landscape pocked with "slave camps under the flag of freedom, massacres justified by philanthropy or by a taste for the superhuman." On the day "when crime dons the apparel of innocence—through a curious transposition peculiar to our times—it is innocence that is called upon to justify itself."[67] Here, for Camus, was the crux of the problem: innocence, or perhaps blamelessness, was at risk. Camus set out to justify not innocence but revolt; to praise not the revolutionary but the rebel. Rebellion alone is the proper response to the betrayal of innocence. It is "born of the spectacle of irrationality confronted with an unjust and incomprehensible condition.... It protests, it demands, it insists that the outrage be brought to an end, and that what has up to now been built upon shifting sands should henceforth be founded on rock."[68]

During the winter of 1946–1947, Camus spent several weeks of convalescence for his tuberculosis in an otherwise empty Alpine hotel. Alone and isolated, Camus worked on *The Rebel* during the day—a project that often left him in despair: "After a week of solitude, again keen awareness of my inadequacy for the work I have begun with the maddest of ambitions. Temptation to give it up." At night, he turned to Montaigne's essays. The choice could not have been coincidental. Montaigne wrote in the midst of the wars of religion, when France was divided as it was during Camus's own day; his essays lambaste both sides for their common conviction that each alone holds the truth. In his longest essay, *Apology for Raymond Sebond*, Montaigne declares a plague on both houses: "See the horrible impudence with which we bandy divine reasons about, and how irreligiously we have both rejected them and taken them again, according as fortune has changed our place in these public storms."[69] Man cannot rise, Montaigne concludes, "above himself and humanity; for he can see only with his own eyes, and seize only with his own grasp."[70] While his contemporaries assumed that this implied the necessity of faith, Camus (and Montaigne) disagreed: it implied, instead, the recognition of limits.

The spirit of Thucydides also hovers over *The Rebel*. In his essay, Camus explores the Thucydidean insights he had earlier used in *The Plague*. The two works offer stunningly similar portrayals of the human predicament, dwelling not just on man's impulse to overreach but also on his reflex to resist when he is the victim of such overreaching. The Athenians overreached at Melos, and the Melians resisted, just as two generations before the Persians had overreached against the Athenians, and the Athenians had in turn resisted. Of course, the Athenian gamble succeeded while the Melian gamble failed—but this is irrelevant. What is relevant is the conviction, shared by Thucydides and Camus, that the desire to resist—to revolt—is no less inherent a human trait than is the drive to dominate. Equally important, revolt creates unity where disunity had once existed. The Greek city-states warred among themselves prior to the Persian invasion, just as the city-states in Sicily did before the Athenians tried to conquer them. So, too, with the resistance movements in France: historical and ideological differences meant little when the nation itself was in danger.

When, at the start of *The Rebel*, Camus declares that the "astonishing history evoked here is the history of European pride," he takes a page from Thucydides' work.[71] At the beginning of his history,

Thucydides states that he will recount the "greatest disturbance in the history of the Hellenes." By book's end, his meaning is clear: it was the "greatest disturbance" because it was the most tragic. Not only was the war fratricidal, pitting Greek against Greek, but it also resulted from man's misplaced confidence in human reason and power. Just like the Athenians at Melos, modern revolutionaries believe they grasp the logic of human nature. The terrorists of the French Revolution, or the Communists of the Russian Revolution, sacrificed others in their belief in historical determinism and the general will. Whoever disagreed was, by definition, a traitor to the nation and to history. With the events of 1789 and 1917, abstractions eclipsed individuals, dreams of totality suppressed the inevitability of differences. Modern revolution, Camus contended, ushered humankind into "the reign of history." While our eyes are fixed on a future of universal brotherhood, our hands stifle and kill others in the present. The ends, no matter how horrific, justify the means. The logic of historical events, "from the moment it is totally accepted, gradually leads it...to mutilate man more and more and to transform itself into objective crime."[72]

For Camus, our present predicament could not be grimmer: on the one hand, we submit to a divine being or a divinized history; on the other hand, we reconcile ourselves to an indifferent sky and an impassible world. While Camus refused the former, he was uncertain if the latter was a basis for an ethics. On the contrary, did it not lay the foundation for the nihilism into which his "German friend" had plunged? Did he not admit that both he and his friend "started out from the same solitude"? Camus of course refused to follow: he never yielded to metaphysical despair. But why choose the path of justice rather than the path of despair? On what ethical grounds did Camus stand, refusing to leap into the void with the nihilist? Even more crucial: Are those grounds strong enough to include others in that same refusal? How can we move from individual to collective revolt?

In *The Myth of Sisyphus,* Camus had insisted that the absurd "does not liberate; it binds. It does not authorize all actions." Though modest, this claim offered a starting point. While the nihilist rejects the very possibility of values, the absurdist thinker insists on their necessity. At first, this sounds like whistling in the dark: if we couch our hope in terms lyrical and desperate enough, we can simply make it so. But it is more than simple whistling—or, rather, the whistling itself points to the *possibility* of harmony. In a way, Camus's claim reflects the belief that if we truly "want an ethical order, [we] are capable of creating one."[73]

From the recognition of absurdity comes revolt; and from revolt comes the recognition that we are not alone. So insistent was Camus on the truth of this claim that he cast it in Cartesian language: "In our daily trials rebellion plays the same role as does the 'cogito' in the realm of thought: it is the first piece of evidence. But this evidence lures the individual from his solitude. It founds its first value on the whole human race. I rebel—therefore we exist."[74] While Camus's statement lacks the a priori rigor of Descartes's cogito, it nevertheless points to an a posteriori truth: across time and place, the act of rebellion reveals certain moral limits common to all human beings. The slave rebels when he has "come to the conclusion that a command has infringed on something in him which does not belong to him alone, but which is common ground where all men—even the man who insults and oppresses him— have a natural community."[75]

The Melians rebelled for the same reason. They embodied Camus's ethical cogito, as the Athenians had before them and the Sicilians would after. Told by the Athenians to submit, the Melians refused: "We are not prepared to give up in a short moment the liberty which our city has enjoyed from its foundation for 700 years."[76] Did Camus have this episode in mind while drafting *The Rebel?* The possibility is intriguing: the dialogue at Melos could certainly have provided Camus with the bridge from solitary to collective rebellion. The anonymous Melians spoke with one voice, united in their act of rebellion. Equally important, their revolt contained its own limits. As the Athenians walked back to their ships, the Melians asked one last time that the two peoples might remain friends. Thucydides reports this remark, or invents it, to underscore a deeper truth. By invoking the theme of friendship, the Melians insisted on the humanity they shared with their enemies, *and that their enemies shared with them.* But the Athenians did not share this sentiment: masters for so long, they saw others as slaves or inferiors.

The Melian offer of friendship to Athens exemplifies the core of Camus's ethical thought: the slave does not deny his master as a fellow human being; he denies him only as his master. The recognition of the master's humanity reminds the slave, no less than the master, of the limits they must observe. This, for Camus, is the "real drama of revolutionary thought": in order to exist, "man must rebel, but rebellion must respect the limits it discovers in itself—a limit where minds meet and, in meeting, begin to exist."[77]

This kind of drama, however, always veers toward tragedy: humankind is incapable of accepting its limits. Camus turned to ancient history for his illustration: Xerxes' whipping of the Bosphorus when a storm delayed his invasion of Greece. "The acme of excess to the Greek mind was to beat the sea with rods—an act of insanity worthy only of barbarians."[78] This gesture shocked the Athenians, yet their descendants were no better than the Persians. Forgetful of their own rebellious past, indifferent to their foes' humanity, convinced they were history's agents, the Athenians at Melos were blindsided by reason and confidence. So too with modern revolutionaries: they were once rebels, resisting others who sought to oppress them. But the oppressed eventually forgot their origins and became in their turn the oppressor.

Could a balance have been found between the daring of the Athenians at Marathon, when they rebelled against the Persian threat, and their presumption at Melos, when they led others to rebel against them? Between the claims of justice that marked Athens' rise and the dangers of limitless liberty that made for its decline? Thucydides raised these questions but offered no answer, for the tragic reason that no answer exists. The same tragic situation frames *The Rebel*. Rebellious thought, Camus wrote, "cannot dispense with memory: it is a perpetual state of tension. In studying its actions and its results, we shall have to say...whether it remains faithful to its noble promise or if, through indolence or folly, it forgets its original purpose and plunges into a mire of tyranny or servitude."[79] Like Thucydides, Camus affirmed the necessity of balance or measure yet concluded that measure must sooner or later falter. By *la mesure,* Camus did not mean a simple reconciliation of contraries. Instead, it was "nothing other than the willing acceptance of contradiction." We must live our lives with this tension. If we ignore or dismiss it, we will lurch "beyond the frontier where opposites balance each other."[80]

○ ○ ○

This tragic tension exists not just among peoples but also between individuals. By 1952, Sartre had ended his long-standing ambivalence towards communism, finally siding with Moscow. He was convinced that "circumstances can sometimes steal our transcendence from us; in that case no individual salvation is possible, only a collective struggle."[81] As if he were exhorting himself, he wrote: "Like it or not, the construction of socialism is privileged in that to understand it one must espouse the movement and adopt its goals."[82] In his private journal, he added: "After ten years of rumination, I had reached a breaking point: one light tap was all that was required."[83]

More precisely, it was a series of taps: the trial of Henri Martin, a Communist French sailor arrested for opposing the war in Indochina; the government's harassment of PCF leaders; the outlawing of a planned demonstration protesting France's participation in NATO; and the publication of *The Rebel*. For Sartre, it was too much to bear: "An anticommunist is a rat. I couldn't see any way out of that one, and I never will.... In the name of those principles that it had inculcated into me, in the name of humanism and of its 'humanities,' in the name of liberty, equality and fraternity, I swore to the bourgeoisie a hatred that would die only with me."[84] Sartre had surrendered to a starkly simple interpretation of political events: one was either for communism, despite its flaws of execution, or liberalism, flawed in its very conception; either for the Soviet Union, despite its concentration camps, or the United States, built by the sweat and labor of slaves and immigrants. Sartre concluded not only that he had no choice but the path of communism but also that all those who did not make the same choice were his objective enemies.

As a consequence, by April 1952, when Sartre and Camus met at a café on the Place Saint-Sulpice, the author of *The Rebel* must have been a reactionary species of vermin in his friend's eyes. While Sartre had not said as much to Camus, he now felt deeply ill at ease with him. While the small man gripped his pipe, Camus sat across the table, wanly joking about the reviews his book had gotten since its publication nearly six months before—reviews, Camus confessed to another friend, that had made him "nauseous and unsteady."[85] Sartre did not know how to reply, in part because of his own attitude toward the book, an attitude he now aligned with his new interpretation of current events.

There was another reason for his discomfort: Sartre had already assigned the book review to a young man named Francis Jeanson. Like Camus, Jeanson had tuberculosis; and like Camus, he disliked the PCF. But unlike Camus, Jeanson owed his career to Sartre: his first book was on Sartre's work, and Sartre thought well enough of Jeanson's ability to hire him, in 1951, to be managing editor of *Les Temps Modernes.* Less than a year later, Sartre asked Jeanson to write the review, claiming he had done so because he believed Jeanson was less hostile to Camus than the other editors. Once he saw Jeanson's draft, however, Sartre was shocked, shocked. Jeanson had written the review, he later recalled, "in the way I had not wanted, that is to say, it was violent and slashing, and it pointed out the book's faults, which was not difficult to do."[86]

Yet as Sartre must have known, Jeanson's review pointed less to the book's faults than to those of the *author:* real, exaggerated, or imagined. At the start, he noted maliciously the applause given to the book by conservatives: "If I were Camus, I'd be worried."[87] He then doubled down: allowing that many on the non-Communist Left also admired the book, Jeanson wondered if this universal approbation was a result of the essay's very vagueness. A Rorschach test for the bourgeois reader who could find whatever she pleased— or, more accurately, whatever pleased her. Most telling was the title given to Jeanson's review: "Albert Camus—Or the Revolted Soul." In casting Camus, the author of *L'homme révolté,* as *l'âme révolté,* Jeanson punned on the French words "man" and "soul." This was a pointed allusion, at least for those acquainted with German idealist philosophy, to G. W. F. Hegel's notion of the "beautiful soul." For Hegel, a "beautiful soul," in its futile attempt to remain pure in the churn of History, inevitably undermines itself. No one, Jeanson lectured Camus, can remain above the political fray. To think otherwise was proof of "that Manichaeism which situates evil within history and good outside it"—nothing less than an "objectively reactionary" choice.[88] In a word, if you are not with us, you must be against us.

The review stunned Camus. He was bruised by the derisive and mocking tone, as he was by the fact that Sartre himself had not reviewed the book. Instead, he had given the task to a young unknown whose obscurity was for Camus "probably the greatest of insults."[89] Enraged and hurt, Camus concluded that Jeanson was little more than a messenger, and that the message was, in fact, from Sartre. While Sartre did not write the review, he must have agreed with it. Otherwise, Camus believed, it would never have seen the light of day.

Acting on this conviction, Camus feverishly drafted a reply. He first addressed it to Jeanson but then struck out the young critic's name, replacing it with "Monsieur le Directeur."[90] He had no doubt, Camus affirmed, that Sartre was *solidaire* with Jeanson's attack. And so Camus had decided to call out Sartre, ensuring the catastrophe for which he had long been waiting. He brushed aside Jeanson's citations of positive critiques from the conservative press—"If the Right possessed the truth, I'd join them"—and claimed the review misrepresented not just *The Rebel* but *The Plague* as well. His aims in both works were so clear, Camus asserted, that one had to be "lying or dreaming" to claim otherwise.[91] Again and again, he accused *Les Temps Modernes*—and, ultimately, Sartre himself—of bad faith: Why bother reviewing a book "if one is determined not to acknowledge what one reads there"? When I "state that the sky is blue, yet you pretend that I said it was black, I have no choice but to conclude that either I am mad or you are deaf."[92]

And yet the sky's real color was there for all to see. Camus had never denied history, as *Les Temps Modernes* claimed, but instead denounced the exaltation of history by Marxism, which transformed a chance series of events into an absolute value, an end that justifies any and all means. More important, *Les Temps Modernes* never bothered to take up Camus's fundamental question: If we accept the historical determinism inherent to Marxist theory, must we not also accept the existence of political tyranny? The reality of the labor camps and show trials and mass purges in the Soviet Union, Camus concluded, could only mean the answer was no. This is why, he affirmed, the "article cannot deal directly with the actual text and must, in order to criticize it, replace it with another."[93]

In the letter's closing lines, Camus shifted from the political to the personal. "I am growing rather tired of seeing myself, and especially of seeing veteran militants who never ran from struggles in their own time, receive countless lessons in effectiveness from critics who have done nothing more than point their seats in the direction of history."[94] As Sartre must have known, this was aimed squarely at him: the joke between friends had now become a barb between foes, and the joyous encounter at the Comédie Française had been eclipsed by an angry confrontation on the stage of public opinion.

o o o

"My dear Camus, our friendship was not an easy one, but I shall miss it. If you break it today, it is certainly because it had to break....Unfortunately you singled me out so deliberately and in so unpleasant a tone that I cannot remain silent without losing face."[95] In his reply to Camus's letter, also published in the August 1952 issue of *Les Temps Modernes,* Sartre took up where Camus had left off: he turned a private and philosophical disagreement into a public and personal confrontation. France had witnessed other clashes, notably the "great noise" of the mid-eighteenth century sparked by the publication of letters between Jean-Jacques Rousseau and David Hume. Then as now, intimate friends became fierce foes and the line collapsed between private concerns and public affairs because the antagonists were not just seminal thinkers but public celebrities. The brilliant, bitter words exchanged between the two figures were broadcast across Europe. Moreover, in both the Age of Enlightenment and the age of existentialism, philosophy was a profession unlike any other: it was a way of life, not a way to make a living. It entailed an accord between thought and action, books written and lives lived.[96]

Sartre's letter was, in a way, as violent and dramatic as Orestes' fatal gestures in *The Flies*. He lashed out at his old friend, ridiculing his vanity and self-righteousness, his posturing and glibness. "A mixture of somber self-conceit and vulnerability has always discouraged anyone from telling you whole truths. The result is that you have become the victim of a bleak immoderation which masks your internal difficulties and which you call, I believe, Mediterranean measure. Sooner or later someone would have told you; let it be me."[97]

Sartre then carried Jeanson's harsh, but false, either/or critique to its logical conclusion: Camus, he declared, was himself an obstacle to history's progress. "You decided against history; and rather than interpret its course, you preferred to see it only as one more absurdity." This would not do: "To merit the right to influence men who are struggling, one must first participate in their struggle, and this first means accepting many things if you hope to change a few of them."[98] By "many things," Sartre must have meant Stalin's crimes, which he had himself denounced in earlier articles. But he got no further in answering Camus's fundamental question: Does working toward a future paradise justify mass murder and slavery in the present?

Underlying Sartre's twenty-page response was a sense of loss and betrayal. He believed that not only had history lost an ally in Camus but that he himself had lost the best of friends. In this light, the letter was less the work of a hostile critic than that of a spurned lover: "You had been for us—and you could be again tomorrow—the admirable conjunction of a person, an action and a work. This was in 1945. We discovered Camus, the Resistant, as we discovered Camus, the author of [*The Stranger*]....You were a real *person*, the most complex and the richest, the last and the most gifted heir of Chateaubriand and the scrupulous defender of the social cause."[99] Perhaps Sartre was not sincere in his wish that Camus once again become what he once had been: he had, after all, condemned Camus to the camp of anti-Communists. But his portrait of the younger Camus was heartfelt: "How we loved you then!"[100]

The August issue of *Les Temps Modernes* hit the newsstands at the onset of *la rentrée*, when vacationing families return from the shores and mountains to their classrooms and offices. The timing swelled public fascination with the quarrel. Screaming from *Samedi-Soir*, a popular tabloid, was the headline: "The Sartre-Camus Break Is Consummated." Underneath were several columns of particularly juicy quotations from the literary exchange, while on the opposite page were racy photos of scantily clad women.[101] Though *Le Monde* and the rest of the serious media latched onto the affair without accompanying pinup photos, they too were as mesmerized by the clash of personalities as by the collision of ideas. How could they not be? Yet underlying the sensational aspect of the clash was the understanding that more was at stake than personal reputations. One paper, *L'Observateur*, noted that the antagonists embodied "two attitudes toward the world," while *Combat* described it as a collision between "two ways of dealing with life."[102]

Camus was deeply shaken by Sartre's letter and horrified that the dispute had become a spectacle—a boxing match, according to some observers, which Sartre had clearly won on points. Camus was greeted with awkward silence or, more often, silent satisfaction by those who felt he had been taken down a notch or two.

To Francine, Camus expressed his greatest insecurities and anguish. Sartre and Jeanson's replies, he told his wife, were insulting and vicious, a "long discussion of my pride which, moreover, has been deeply bruised....I am paying a great price for this unfortunate book. Today I doubt everything in it just as I doubt my own self which so closely resembles it."[103] A few days later, Camus was even gloomier: "I've been alone with bleak and numbing thoughts," he confided to Francine. He was, he wrote, doing his best to come to terms with a bad situation, much "the way one makes do in an uncomfortable bed." While his book was of course open to discussion, it was his own character that instead was being attacked: "Most striking is this explosion of long simmering hatred, proof that these people were never my friends and that my beliefs have always bothered them." He refused to respond to the attacks and worried only about how to "distinguish truth from falsehood in all of this muck."[104]

Camus also spilled his anguish onto the pages of his journal. Even before the publication of *The Rebel*, he had questioned the book and himself: he hated how Paris had changed him, held "the most dreadful opinion" of himself, repeatedly quoted Ralph Waldo Emerson and Henry David Thoreau on self-reliance, and castigated the press for its cruelty and glibness. "In France today," he wrote, the "simple suspicion of intelligence is enough to sink a man." As the quarrel gained speed, Camus's thoughts darkened: "The one thing that has always saved me amid all my prostrations is that I have never stopped believing in what, for lack of anything better, I will call 'my star.' But today, I no longer believe in it." Never had he felt so alone: "Every man and woman against me, to destroy me, seeking their share without respite, without ever, ever lending a hand, coming to my aid, loving me for what I am so that I may remain what I am."[105]

o o o

In Aeschylus's *Oresteia,* Orestes makes his way back to Argos, uncertain and alone. Describing his life as a "trial," he tells his sister Electra:

> For such as us, no share in the wine-bowl
> no libations poured in love...
> There is no refuge, none to take you in.
> A pariah, reviled, at long last you die
> withered in the grip of all this dying.

Camus's predicament was much less tragic than Orestes'. He was not alone: expressions of support and admiration were numerous, though, tellingly, many came from expatriate writers such as Czeslaw Milosz, Witold Gombrowicz, and Hannah Arendt. And lives were not at stake, only reputations and self-esteem, small beer compared to the destiny thrust on Orestes.

Yet Aeschylus's tragedy illuminates an essential element of the confrontation between Camus and Sartre. At the beginning of the tragedy, Agamemnon finds himself caught in an impossible position: he must obey Zeus's command and lead his fleet to Troy; but the fleet can sail only if, as Artemis demands, Agamemnon first sacrifices his daughter Iphigenia. Agamemnon cries out, "Pain both ways and what is worse?" In the end, he sacrifices his child. He "slip[s] his neck in the strap of Fate" and now refers to Iphigenia as a "yearling." The pitch of horror reaches its height when he cuts her throat as if she were an animal. The fleet sails, lands at Troy, and the rest is the stuff of mythology.

But the rest is also the stuff of ethics. Agamemnon's choices are limited and equally grim: he seems to have no option but to align himself with necessity. But as the philosopher Martha Nussbaum notes, from the moment Agamemnon makes his terrifying decision, "he strangely turns himself into a collaborator, a willing victim."[106]

He transforms himself from father into executioner, human being into instrument, tormented into tormentor. Even more than his own re-creation of Orestes in *The Flies*, who relishes and realizes himself through an act of violence, Sartre resembled Aeschylus's Agamemnon. Like Agamemnon, who bends his own will in the direction of destiny, Sartre decided he had no choice but to align himself with the direction of History. Like Agamemnon, who embraces perceived necessity with inhuman fury, Sartre threw himself into the class struggle with terrifying ferocity. And like Agamemnon, who broke the bonds of loyalty and expelled Iphigenia from the company of human beings, Sartre betrayed his friendship with Camus, consigning him to the class of anti-Communist rats.

The most crucial moment of *The Libation Bearers*—the second play in the *Oresteia* trilogy—is when Orestes, poised to kill his mother, hesitates. Knife in hand, he turns to his friend Pylades: "What will I do, Pylades: I dread to kill my mother!" Pylades does not pause: "Make all mankind your enemy, not the gods." Sartre agreed: better to serve his gods—History—than attend to individuals. As he boasted to Camus, he had dirty hands: "Right up to the elbows. I've plunged them in filth and blood. But what do you hope? Do you think you can govern innocently?" When he closed the books on his friendship with Camus, Sartre thus echoed Agamemnon's cry: "Law is law! Let all go well..."[107]

Sartre's certitude appalled Camus: the *pied noir* refused to quit the space between Orestes' question and Pylades' reply. Instead, Camus claimed the sacred ground of hesitation: only there do we have the space necessary to understand the tragic complexities of life. This is also the perspective of Aeschylean tragedy, in which so-called solutions do not solve the problem. Instead, they "simply underdescribe or misdescribe it." The best we can do, the closest we can get to a solution, is "to describe and see the conflict clearly."[108]

Such a description deprives us of metaphysical or ideological solace, but this is a good, even great thing. A life empty of transcendental guidance, a life that assumes responsibility for its choices, a life that knows the importance of clearly stating the problem is a life alert to the dangers of launching oneself blindly into a solution. We must live our lives, in the end, aware of our language and our limits. In a reply he wrote to Sartre's letter, Camus affirmed that humankind, if it hopes to remain humane, "must maintain itself at the very limits of revolt, where heartbreak and lucidity are one. Short of, or beyond this limit, struggle no longer exists. There is only consent and, in a sense, passivity."[109] As it turned out, Camus never sent the letter. Lucid and heartbroken, he understood there was no need to do so.

CHAPTER FOUR

1956

SILENCE FOLLOWS

The criticism of language cannot get around the fact that our words commit us and that we should remain faithful to them. Naming an object inaccurately means adding to the unhappiness of the world.

On Sunday afternoon, January 22, 1956, thousands of Algerians—European and Arab—thronged the Place du Gouvernement in Algiers. Leading the *pieds noirs* was a local bar owner and brawler, Jo Ortiz. He was a die-hard *ultra,* the name given to those for whom Algeria would always be part of France, who believed that the privileges long enjoyed by the *pieds noirs* should never be taken away. On the other side, members of the Front de Libération Nationale (FLN), the underground movement dedicated to Algeria's independence, maintained control of the Arab crowd. Dividing the two hostile groups was a thin cordon of gendarmes, commanded by the city's prefect.

The backdrop to the event was the grand building known as the Cercle du Progrès. Built by a reformist Muslim organization in the

1930s, this meeting hall straddled two worlds. Behind it spilled the Kasbah, the ancient Muslim district laced with alleys and passages; in front sprawled Bab el-Oued, a working-class neighborhood dominated by Spanish immigrants. In its way, the building was a fitting site for that day's event. At two o'clock, Albert Camus was scheduled to appear. He had just flown to Algiers to urge the warring peoples to accept a civil truce. A few days before, he wrote in his journal that his decision to go home had lifted a great weight from his shoulders: "Only risk justifies thought. And then anything is better than this France of resignation and brutality, this swamp where I suffocate. Yes, I arose happy, for the first time in months. I've recovered the star."[1]

Camus now doubted this earlier élan. He looked around the mobbed hall, filled with Europeans and Arabs who he believed were condemned to live together, while outside those same peoples seemed destined to go on killing one another. Since his arrival four days earlier, Camus had been bombarded with death threats, along with appeals from friends asking him to leave his hotel for the safety of their homes. Inside the hall, brawny friends from Camus's old neighborhood of Belcourt surrounded him: with a wan smile, he referred to them as his "gorillas." He had cast himself in an impossible role—mediator between two nations at war with each other. Gripping the text of his speech, his face pale, Camus faced the climax of a tragedy worthy of Aeschylus or Thucydides.

o o o

Massacres had marked the evolution of the war in Algeria. It came to life in 1945 at Sétif, a modest town in Kabylia that harbored a small European community. On May 8, 1945, the *pieds noirs* prepared to celebrate the end of World War II. So, too, did the Muslim population, but for very different reasons. Poor harvests and a wartime rationing system favoring the *pieds noirs* had worsened already tense relations between the two communities. For the Muslims, V-E Day provided an ideal opportunity to call for national independence. Were not France and the rest of the world celebrating their own liberation after years of brutal occupation? How could the French not see that the values for which they had fought and died were no less legitimate for those who considered France an occupier in their own land?

The nationalist demonstration quickly collapsed into a bloodbath. Somewhere, someone fired a shot; guns and knives replaced banners and flags. By the end of the day, the rampaging protesters overwhelmed the small police force and murdered more than one hundred French residents. While there are no clean massacres, this one was especially horrific: women's breasts were sliced off, men's genitals were stuffed into their mouths. The French state's response was equally appalling: waves of organized repression and vigilante violence washed over the region for the next several days. Upwards of fifteen thousand Arabs and Berbers were killed, often in grisly fashion. The enormity of the repression bought a decade of uneasy peace, but the price was high: clear-sighted observers understood that a line had been crossed in 1945.

While the French press generally played down the violence at Sétif, the political parties lamented the *pied noir* deaths and ignored the subsequent massacre of Muslims. Even the Communists, lulled by the myth of assimilation, were shocked by the religious and nationalist character of the rebellion. Camus's old friend Amar Ouzegane, the leader of the Algerian Communist Party, denounced the rebellion and demanded that its ringleaders be "swiftly and pitilessly punished."[2]

Camus had flown to Algeria shortly before the bloody events of May: for the first time since the Occupation he could see his family. But there was also a pressing professional reason: he was determined to pick up where he had left off in 1939 with his series of reports on Kabylia. While he planned a similar "investigation" of conditions among the Arab and Berber populations, Camus was no longer an obscure journalist for *Alger-Républicain*. He was editor of France's most prestigious newspaper, *Combat*, and one of the country's most prominent intellectuals.[3] Equally important, Camus was about to discover that Algeria was no longer the same country it had been in 1939: the experiences of war and liberation had galvanized the political expectations of its Arab and Berber populations, while hardening the resistance of its European settlers.

Despite the volatile conditions, Camus spent most of April crisscrossing Algeria, traveling the length of the coast and descending more than five hundred miles toward the desert. Though he returned to Paris on May 8 or shortly before, Camus clearly anticipated the nationalist explosion in his native land. Below the bold headline "Crisis in Algeria," his first article appeared in the May 13 edition of *Combat*. Warning of the "grave difficulties with which Algeria is grappling today," he proceeded to give his readers a primer in geography, demography, and history. Little had changed in the conditions of the rural population since his earlier visit to Kabylia: too little food for too many mouths, too many republican ideals given the lie by selfish *pieds noirs* and feckless French administrators. The reality of the rationing system was stark: *pieds noirs* were entitled to 300 grams of bread per day, while Arabs and Berbers usually received fewer than 150 grams per day. This staggering inequality was being imposed on people who not only "are not inferior except in regard to the conditions in which they must live," but who also "have spent the past two years fighting for the liberation of France." France's duty was clear: it had to "quell the cruelest of hungers and heal inflamed hearts."[4]

As he had in 1939, Camus insisted on the universal quality of human dignity, all the while holding on to the particularity of individual human beings. All of us, he told his readers, were duty-bound to "understand [the Algerian Muslims] before we judge them."[5] While the crisis was most immediately economic and material, he continued, its roots were political and historical. For more than a century, France had failed to apply its democratic principles to Algeria's native peoples. For this reason, France would have to "conquer Algeria a second time."[6] Camus's provocative declaration underscored a prosaic truth: the ideals of the republic extended no further than the European havens in Algeria. If Algeria were to remain part of France, France had to reconquer it not by force of arms but instead by the systematic and sincere application of the rights, duties, and benefits of citizenship. In his final editorial, Camus declared: "Our feverish and unbridled desire for power and expansion will never be excused unless we make up for them by unwavering attention to the pursuit of justice and the spirit of self-sacrifice. Despite the repressive actions we have just taken in North Africa, I am convinced that the era of Western imperialism is over."[7]

Camus rightly forecast the eclipse of imperialism. France had been weakened by the costs of war, occupation, and liberation; the nation no longer had the economic or material means to maintain its empire. Moreover, its political and moral claims had been undermined not just by France's unwillingness to implement its own promises in Algeria but also by the growth of pan-Arab nationalism. The problem, Camus noted, was "quite simply that time marches on."[8]

He grasped far better than most of his contemporaries that *Combat*'s slogan, "From Resistance to Revolution," had inspired not just men and women living under the Nazi occupation but also men and women living under French colonial rule. The French civilizing mission could only be fulfilled, he announced, by bringing "more complete liberation to everyone it subjugates." If France failed to do so, it would "reap hatred like all vanquishers who prove themselves incapable of moving beyond victory." Camus's warning not to repeat the experience France had had under the Nazi occupation was remarkable: few on the Left, much less the Right, cast French actions in such terms. More remarkable, however, was his call for justice, despite the blood that had just been shed. "Unfortunate and innocent French victims have lost their lives, and this crime in itself is inexcusable. But I hope that we will respond to murder with nothing other than justice, so as to avoid doing irreparable harm."[9] Here again, Camus's allegiance to moderation—the balance dear to the ancient Greeks—was striking. Like Aeschylus's Athena, who urges the Furies to give up their desire for vengeance and to avoid any action that "strikes a note of brutal conquest," Camus asked that all men embrace justice and, as Athena pleaded, "revere the Mean."[10]

Yet the irreparable had already been done in Camus's Algeria, if not in Aeschylus's Athens. Camus's belief that it was not too late to salvage a fully democratic and egalitarian French Algeria, while well-founded in the 1930s, bordered on nostalgia by the mid-1950s. The sails of Arab nationalism were beginning to fill—represented most notably by Gamal Abdel Nasser's rise in Egypt—and most *pieds noirs* were growing increasingly fearful. That community had rejected earlier opportunities, most importantly the Blum-Viollette proposal in 1936, and continued to resist efforts at compromise after 1945. By then, however, their obstructionism was simply worsening a situation they had already whipped toward a violent end.

Still, Camus insisted that both sides, even after Sétif, could still be persuaded to embrace the mean: his own past told him he was right. His childhood experiences were powerful testimony to the reality of republican egalitarianism. Taken in charge by teachers such as Louis Germain, men who were committed to the ideal of republican education, a fatherless and dirt-poor Camus made his way through the *lycée* and university. The French republic had taken this working-class child's native intelligence and talent, drive and curiosity, and had turned him into a Frenchman. In the novel he would never complete, *The First Man*, Camus recalls sitting at his desk in the spare classroom in Algiers, where the students—who knew only "the sirocco and the dust"—read "stories that to them were mythical." They were based in "France," a land of snow and smoking chimneys, mysterious traditions and exotic customs. These accounts, of course, were "part of the poetry of school," but they were also part of a curriculum whose ideal was based on the universal values of 1789.[11] When Camus asked if France "attributed to its democratic principles a value *universal enough*" to extend them to the Muslim peoples of Algeria, he was utterly sincere.[12] The path to a better future for all Algerians depended on education—a belief that spurred Camus's outraged observation that more than a million Muslim children were without schools.[13]

o o o

The young Camus's education came not only from French republican primers and school exercises. There were also the lessons provided by a harsh life: as Camus told a critic who belittled his knowledge of Marxist theory, his teacher had been *la misère*, not Marx's books.[14] Tragically, the vast majority of Muslims in Algeria could make the same claim. Camus's belief in the transformative power of republican education, still defensible in 1945, had by 1956 been irrevocably overtaken by events: European and Muslim Algerians had learned their lessons in the misery of civil war.

That education had begun little more than a year before in Philippeville, a port on Algeria's upper coast. Unlike Sétif, where the nightmarish events began spontaneously, the FLN—not yet created in 1945—deliberately chose Philippeville as the stage for its blood-spattered rebellion. Unable to defeat the French militarily, the FLN leadership decided to terrorize French civilians. One FLN leader, Youssef Zighout, told his men that in response to the "collective repression" of the French state, they must "reply with collective reprisals against Europeans, military and civil, who are all united behind the crimes committed on our people. For them, no pity, no quarter."[15]

Zighout's watchwords were applied meticulously in Philippeville. In early August 1955, FLN units descended on the *pied noir* communities in and around the town and systematically slaughtered more than one hundred men, women, and children. The FLN did not work alone: many local Muslim men, who had worked side by side with the *pieds noirs* for years, joined the massacre, while Muslim women lifted their voices in unearthly chants of "you-you." As at Sétif, the French reaction was indiscriminate and wildly lopsided: army units fired at will into crowds in which rebels were indistinguishable from civilians, and vigilante groups formed with the government's blessing murdered dozens of locals. When the French government announced the body count, 71 French civilian deaths were placed on the scales against 1,273 FLN deaths, according to French authorities. According to the FLN, however, more than 12,000 Muslim men, women, and children were killed in the massive French reaction.[16]

In *The Plague,* Tarrou does not distinguish among the dead. "All I maintain," he tells Rieux, "is that on this earth there are pestilences and there are victims, and it's up to us, so far as possible, not to join forces with the pestilences." Anticipating the cynical shrug of realists, he adds: "That may sound simple to the point of childishness; I can't judge if it's simple, but I know it's true."[17] For several months, Camus had used his public celebrity to apply Tarrou's ethic to Algeria's worsening situation. In an open letter to an

Algerian friend, the Socialist Aziz Kessous, Camus acknowledged that the events in Philippeville had pushed him to the "verge of despair." How could it be otherwise? "We know nothing of the human heart," he wrote, "if we imagine that the Algerian French can now forget the massacres at Philippeville and elsewhere." But he did not stop there: "And it is another form of madness to imagine that repression can make the Arab masses feel confidence and esteem for France."

And yet, neither the European nor the Arab community could will the other to disappear. While Tarrou fears that his ethic will strike realists as "childish," Camus now argued that it was true childishness to believe that this truth could be washed away in a great wave of blood. The "French fact," Camus declared, "cannot be eliminated in Algeria, and the dream of a sudden disappearance of France is childish." No less puerile, however, was the wish of some French Algerians to "cancel out, silence and subjugate" 9 million Muslims. French and Muslims, he insisted, were "condemned to live together." This, Camus felt, meant that men of goodwill on both sides had to risk death to secure a space where the "exchange of views is still possible."[18]

Camus began to build a case for a civil truce in a series of editorials for the liberal French journal *L'Express*. In calling for a roundtable at which all the factions would sit down together, Camus showed his hand: the antagonists, facing one another, would have to attend to one another. This might, Camus thought, give a "meaning to the fighting—and perhaps render it pointless."[19] It was the same ethical reflex that, in 1939, had prompted Camus to ask his paper's readers to see the humanity of the shipbound Arab prisoners and to ask the governor general of Algeria—a man hidden behind the pomp and circumstance of his office—to see the humanity of Michel Hodent, wrongly accused by the judicial system. It was this same reflex, in 1945, that led Camus, after a sleepless night, to affirm the humanity of Robert Brasillach. Just as he saw that his whole effort then, "whatever the situation, misfortune or disillusion, must be to make contact again," so too did he insist that the antagonists in 1955 make contact, if only across a table.[20]

The cascade of editorials climaxed in early January 1956 with Camus's outline for a civil truce. Deploring the deaths of French and Muslim civilians, condemning the habit on each side of holding only the other responsible, Camus declared: "Soon only the dead will be innocent." He demanded that both sides denounce the violence aimed at all civilians. He urged the *pieds noirs* to "recognize what is just in your adversary's cause, as well as what is not just in your own repressive measures." And he made the very same demand of the FLN: "Disavow the murder of innocents." Before the situation became yet more catastrophic, both sides had to agree to spare civilians. "We must all demand a truce—a truce that will allow us to arrive at solutions, a truce regarding the massacre of civilians by both sides."[21]

In the last lines, Camus called on his readers to rally behind the French and Algerian moderates—"movements [are] taking shape everywhere"—dedicated to dialogue. Camus's desperate lyricism got the better of him: "everywhere" was limited to precious few places in Algeria, while there was only one movement, singular in every sense of the word. Camus was aware of its fragility, for he had himself been in contact with it for several days. Its nucleus was the Association of Friends of Arabic Theater, *pieds noirs* and Muslims who shared a common love of theater. Among the members were Jean de Maisonseul, Charles Poncet, and Louis Miquel, veterans of the Théâtre du Travail and the Théâtre l'Equipe, all members of *la bande à Camus*. On the Muslim side were, most important, Amar Ouzegane and Mohammed Lebjaoui. Twenty years earlier, Ouzegane had been Camus's sympathetic mentor in the Algerian Communist Party; like Camus, Ouzegane was eventually expelled from its ranks. By 1955, however, and unknown to Camus, Ouzegane had, like the other Muslim participants in the theater group, gone over to the FLN.

In the 1930s, moral and political ideals had inspired Camus and his friends to take to the stage; as their manifesto grandly declared, art must "descend from its ivory tower" at times of crisis. The necessity was even greater in 1956. And so, when the group got in touch with Camus with the idea of a joint political action in Algiers, he agreed. But there were huge question marks. Just as the working-class audience for the Travail and Equipe groups never materialized, it was not at all clear if the intended audience—moderate and liberal *pieds noirs* and Muslims—for this different kind of performance even existed. And if they did, would they be willing to turn out for this unprecedented performance?

Moreover, the group's preparations for the public forum were hardly promising. At a meeting on January 19, an Arab schoolteacher blurted out: "To hell with the civil truce! What we need is absolute and unconditional independence now." Waxen-faced, Camus turned to his friend Louis Miquel: "What the hell am I doing here? We're screwed. Do they really expect us to drop our pants?" At a second meeting, a young Arab insisted that terrorist attacks would end only when France recognized Algeria's independence. When he heard this at the back of the room where he was standing, Camus fell silent and then walked out.[22]

At the same time, Camus was receiving death threats from *pied noir* extremists. As the Sunday event approached, a friendly police official warned the group that extremists were busy forging tickets: they planned to mob the hall and disrupt the proceedings. The group quickly printed new tickets, while the Arab participants assured Camus that they would guarantee security. Violence seemed inevitable; more than once, Camus considered canceling the event.

Yet he persisted: despite his justified suspicions of the FLN's role in his public appearance, despite his shock on seeing how radicalized both sides had become, despite his fear that Paris was willfully blind to the depth of the problem, Camus persisted. The same spirit that precipitated his writings during the Occupation now sped his actions in Algiers. True despair is not born, he believed, when we face a stubborn opponent or in the exhaustion of unequal combat. Instead, despair comes to us "when we no longer know why we are struggling—or, indeed, if struggle is necessary."[23]

o o o

The political situation in Paris, even at this late date, gave Camus reason to continue his fight. President René Coty had dissolved the French National Assembly the previous December, and expectations ran high that Pierre Mendès-France would become the next prime minister. Mendès seemed to be a man apart. He had escaped from a Vichy prison during the war and had become an airman for the Free French. In 1945, de Gaulle had named him to the Ministry of the Economy, from which he resigned a few months later. While the cause was technical—Mendès had unsuccessfully argued for a policy of financial and monetary austerity against the inflationary policies followed by de Gaulle—the underlying reason was ethical. As he told de Gaulle in his letter of resignation: "To distribute money to everyone without taking any back is to foster a mirage...but the more we grant nominal satisfactions, the less we are able to give real satisfactions....I cannot accept solidarity for measures I consider nefarious."[24]

Mendès applied this same rigorous and blunt approach when he returned to political office ten years later. He came to power in the wake of the Battle of Dien Bien Phu, when a French military garrison, after suffering appalling losses, surrendered to the nationalist forces of the Vietminh. Mendès became prime minister in mid-1954, vowing that he would quickly extricate France from Indochina. Within a month, he had made good on his promise and turned his attention to other fissures in the splintering French empire. He flew to Tunisia and set in motion the colony's peaceful transition to independence; the same model would be applied shortly thereafter to Morocco.

Mendès then confronted Algeria, aware that it was a different case altogether. Among his first acts was to send Jacques Soustelle to Algiers as his governor general. A hero of the Resistance and a trained ethnologist, Soustelle was an inspired choice. Equally inspired was Soustelle's decision, soon after arriving in Algeria, to name Germaine Tillion to his administration. Like Soustelle, Tillion was a celebrated member of the Resistance; more important, she too was an ethnologist who had studied the tribes of the Aurès, a barren and mountainous region in southeastern Algeria. Both Soustelle and Tillion were critical of the historical wrongs done to the Arab and Berber peoples and, like Camus, both believed in the republican ideal of integration. But a powerful *pied noir* community determined to maintain the status quo repeatedly stymied Soustelle's efforts at liberalization. Already suspect in the eyes of many *pieds noirs,* Soustelle also failed to win the confidence of the Muslim community. Following the bloodbath at Philippeville, and spurred by the FLN policy of murdering prominent Muslims opposed to their agenda, moderate Muslims soon began to denounce Soustelle's policy of integration and to rally behind the FLN banner.

During the last months of 1954, the government's struggle to hold the middle ground was undone by extremists on both sides. When the government finally collapsed in February 1955, Mendès delivered a prophetic speech. While deputies on both the Left and Right tried to shout him down, Mendès declared that France faced a stark choice: either build "with the Muslim peoples a common edifice, or else the legacy of a century of history will crumble in hatred and bloodshed." As heckling and catcalls drowned out his voice, Mendès remained at the podium. His last words as prime minister were fateful: France's politicians must ultimately give the country "reasons to hope and to overcome the hatred which we have too often made into a spectacle. *Vive la France!*"[25]

Many observers, including Camus, expected Mendès to return to office. It was a realistic expectation but also a fervent hope: he was the one individual, many believed, who could prevent France and Algeria from pulling each other into the abyss. Mendès alone seemed able to master France's unstable parliamentary system, a recipe for public scorn in the best of times and for despair in the worst. By 1955, the worst of the worst seemed to have arrived. The novelist Jean Dutourd described France as a "dying carcass on which her maggot-ministers prosper"—brutal words that found wide acceptance.[26]

Camus had met Mendès just once many years before, but he was deeply impressed: he told a friend, "I felt I had met a true states-man."[27] It was with the hope of returning Mendès to power that Camus joined *L'Express:* the newspaper had gone from a weekly to a daily format with the express aim of electing Mendès. Yet despite the paper's efforts, the campaign fell short of victory. The elections in December 1955 simply moved around the existing political chess pieces, all of which had to make room for the sudden arrival of the Union de Défense des Commerçants et Artisans (UDCA), better known as the Poujadists. Led by their founder, Pierre Pou-jade, the UDCA won more than fifty seats in the assembly, giv-ing national prominence to their antirepublican, anti-Semitic, and anti-Muslim rhetoric. Not surprisingly, Poujade threw his support behind the ultras in Algeria, thus further complicating the politi-cal calculus in Paris. Several weeks of horse-trading followed; as late as January 18, when Camus flew to Algiers, a new government had still not taken office. Finally, on January 25, President René Coty asked the Socialist leader Guy Mollet to form a new government. Mendès was given the position of minister without portfolio, which amounted to little more than minister without influence. His political career had come to an end, as had any realistic hope for a diplomatic settlement in Algeria.

o o o

As Algeria was unraveling in 1954, Camus reflected on "action and writing" in his notebooks. He wondered if "engaged" writers write because they are uncertain about the justness of their engagement. Burdened with a guilty conscience, they thrash around for reasons to justify their engagement—a reflex mirrored by their opponents: "Thus, the positions will stiffen. So many repeated assertions will be equivalent to actions. Will soon provoke them. Thus, the victorious party will have enough charges on the day of victory. By means of continually fleeing their guilty consciences, the losers will have found true guilt and will answer for it, never having wanted that. Another day, the victors, in turn, will be vanquished and will respond, never having wanted that. History is a long crime perpetrated by the innocent."[28]

By the time he stood at the podium in the Cercle de Progrès, Camus faced the real-life consequences of this infernal logic. He believed that both sides were, in a fundamental sense, right; but instead of acknowledging this quandary, each side claimed sole possession of the truth. They had lied about themselves, had lied about their opponents, and were committing real crimes, drowning Algeria in one another's blood.

Behind Camus as he prepared to speak were three members of Algeria's quickly disappearing middle: a Catholic priest, a Protestant minister, and an unofficial representative of the Muslim community, Abdelaziz Khalid. His eyes fastened to the text and his words softly spoken, Camus invoked their presence: "This meeting had to take place to show at least that an exchange of views is still possible." All the committee members were private, not public, figures. But with war now seeping into the realm of the private, these men had stepped forward. They had walked onto this stage in the knowledge that "building, teaching, creating [are] functions of life and of generosity that could not be pursued in the realm of hatred and bloodshed."

We must not deny, Camus continued, fundamental historical and demographic facts. In Algeria "there are a million Frenchmen who have been here for a century, millions of Muslims, either Arabs or Berbers, who have been here for centuries, and several rigorous religious communities." This swath of North African coast, he announced, was the "crossroads" where history had thrown together these various peoples. Yet extremists were trying to throttle this reality by terrorizing not just the other side but also the moderate members of their own ethnic groups. Fleshing out the abstract thoughts he had earlier traced in his notebook, Camus pointed to the spiral of lies and violence sweeping across Algeria. If both sides did not open a dialogue, the Frenchman would make up his mind "to know nothing of the Arab, even though he feels somewhere within him, that the Arab's claim to dignity is justified, and the Arab [would make] up his mind to know nothing of the Frenchman, even though he feels, somewhere within him, that the Algerian French likewise have a right to security and dignity on our common soil." And yet, Camus continued in dismay, each refuses to look at the other. If each and every Frenchman and Muslim did not make an honest "effort to think over his adversary's motives," the violent would carry Algeria away.[29]

Early in his speech, Camus paused when a late-arriving Ferhat Abbas, the great moderate voice of Algerian nationalism, stepped onto the stage. As the two men embraced, the audience cheered. For a moment, the applause calmed the gathering storm outside: for a moment, Camus's plea for a civil truce seemed possible. But stones began to break through the windows, accompanied by calls to lynch Camus. Ortiz had not been idle: he had helped work the *pied noir* protesters into a white fury. Camus began to speak more quickly as he feared the mob was about to burst into the hall and create a bloody ruckus. How absurd, he announced, to appear in this tumult, asking for nothing more than that "a handful of innocent victims [i.e., civilians on both sides] be spared." No less absurdly, his words were blurred by the uproar and his own rushed delivery. Though the committee had planned a public discussion after the speech, Camus asked that it be canceled: it seemed clear as the noise outside grew that the conference would soon give way to disorder and much worse. The visitor left the hall as he had arrived, surrounded by a cordon of childhood friends. Could he have known that his last words—that both sides must refuse to practice and to suffer terror—were as stirring, and futile, as the Melian warnings to the Athenians two millennia before?[30]

The next day, Camus succeeded in meeting with Soustelle on his way to the airport. The conversation was short and unsatisfying. Soustelle was unbending, refusing to allow noncombatant status to men who were civilians by day, terrorists by night.[31] His remark seemed to underscore one of the impracticalities of Camus's appeal: the FLN's strategy dictated precisely the kind of war Soustelle—and Camus—found reprehensible. Given the overwhelming force of the French military, the FLN leaders had deliberately launched a terror campaign aimed at French civilians in the expectation that France would respond with disproportionate force against Muslim civilians. Terror was clearly the order of the day for the Algerian revolutionaries and, seen through the blood-dimmed prism of Philippeville, it seemed to be working.

Camus flew back to Paris later that day, filled with more despair than hope. He had gained a deeper appreciation of the many inequities forced on the Muslim majority and of the iniquities committed by the ultras. He was also unsettled by the isolation of moderates like Abbas, too long disdained by the French and now scorned by a new generation of Algerian militants. (Abbas's nephew had been murdered by the FLN at Philippeville, and Abbas himself joined the organization a few months after Camus's public speech.) Camus tried to maintain an air of determined optimism, insisting he would "sacrifice everything to the truce." In *L'Express*, he declared that his meeting represented a "step forward." But he also confessed he did not know *how* to take the next step: instead of a durable solution, "I have only doubts."[32]

Subsequent events in Paris and Algiers deepened those doubts. Soustelle was recalled to Paris by the Mollet government, which was convinced he had become too beholden to the *pieds noirs*. Georges Catroux, a former military officer and liberal reformer, was named as his replacement. This announcement was the spark that set ablaze the great mass of *pied noir* tinder. When Mollet arrived in Algiers for an official visit on February 5, the fire scorched and nearly killed him. Greeted at the airport by just a few local officials, Mollet was driven into town along deserted roads lined by security forces. His uneasiness grew when he arrived in Algiers: the city was silent and shuttered. It was only when Mollet went to lay a wreath at the city's war memorial that he confronted an even greater mob than had greeted Camus. Once again led by Ortiz, the crowd threatened to hang Mollet. This time, however, they underscored their threats by heaving volleys of rotten vegetables at the official delegation. A great wave of demonstrators surged toward the statue where Mollet stood, splattered and shocked. They crashed against the cordon of riot police; had it not been for additional forces brought from France, they might have burst through and murdered Mollet. Stunned and frightened, the prime minister was hustled away by the police behind a wall of tear gas.

From the safety of the governmental residence, Mollet announced that Catroux had resigned. A deafening cheer rose from the great crush of victorious *pieds noirs.* Mollet thus did what Camus had refused to do two weeks earlier: he abandoned the middle ground of reason and dialogue. In his notebooks, he scrawled a prophetic line: "It seems that in this country no party can sustain the patriotic effort for long. So the right gives up in 1940 and then the left sixteen years later."[33] Already a desperate affair, the cause of a civil truce was buried the next day when Catroux's replacement, Robert Lacoste, refused to meet with Camus's committee.

o o o

In *The Rebel,* Camus discusses a group of remarkable men and women he calls the "fastidious assassins." They were early twentieth-century Russian revolutionaries who tried to overthrow the Czarist regime. For Camus, they were the last of their kind: never again would history see the "spirit of rebellion encountering the spirit of compassion."[34] They were revolutionaries in spite of themselves, dedicated to a cause whose price left them sleepless, haunted by the unforeseen consequences for the innocent. For Camus, the greatest tribute we could pay these men and women is "that we would not be able, in 1950, to ask them one question that they themselves had not already asked and that, in their life or by their death, they had not partially answered."[35]

Such introspection seemed positively quaint in 1956. Yet Camus held fast to this ideal and never abandoned the memory of Ivan Kaliayev. In 1905, Kaliayev had assassinated one of the czar's uncles, Grand Duke Sergei. But he succeeded only on the second try. Kaliayev aborted his first attempt when he saw two children sitting next to the duke in the royal carriage. Kaliayev defused the bomb he was about to throw, saving the lives of the innocent children but endangering his own life and those of fellow conspirators. When Kaliayev finally carried out his plan two days later, he allowed himself to be arrested and walked calmly to his execution.

In his play *The Just Assassins*, Camus explores the ethical nature of Kaliayev's act. After he calls off his first attempt, Kaliayev's fellow revolutionary Stepan berates him. "Children!" he explodes: "There you go, always talking about children!" Because Kaliayev does not throw the bomb, "thousands of Russian children will die of hunger for many years to come." The utilitarian calculus is straightforward: "Not until the day comes when we stop being sentimental about children, will the revolution triumph and we be masters of the world....Nothing that can serve our cause should be ruled out....There are no limits."[36]

The consequences of a world freed from limits had preoccupied Camus for most of his life: he brooded over metaphysical limits in *The Myth of Sisyphus*, moral limits in *Letters to a German Friend*, and political limits in *The Rebel*. With the advent of war in Algeria, Camus now confronted the question of limits in yet another guise. Stepan's moral absolutism in *The Just Assassins* anticipates the rationale offered by European apologists for the FLN's terrorism such as Merleau-Ponty and Sartre. In a way, the case for revolutionary violence made by Merleau-Ponty in *Humanism and Terrorism* was fungible: any revolutionary convinced he is on the right side of history is free to use it. The FLN and its supporters had concluded that violence was part and parcel of historical experience.

For Camus, too many individuals on both sides were guilty not just of murder but also of flattening life into abstractions or stereotypes. In particular, Camus struggled against the Left Bank's simplistic view of the *pieds noirs*. It was not a land of *richards*—wealthy European landowners and industrialists—who carry "riding crops, smoke cigars and drive Cadillacs."[37] Most *pieds noirs* were instead of modest means; it was his family and neighbors in Belcourt, Camus feared, who would pay the heaviest price for the Left's "murderous frivolity."[38] These "intellectuals for progress," Camus despaired, "rethread the stitches of reasoning torn out by...every head that falls."[39]

o o o

Heads were already falling in 1956. His failure as a peacemaker haunted Camus. By the time he left Algeria, he felt he had been used by the FLN, whose role he discovered only after the fact. Yet, once Camus was back in France, he found that former friends on the Left saw his efforts as little more than grandstanding. Beauvoir spoke for the circle at *Les Temps Modernes* when she defended the FLN's use of terrorism—"We refused to feel indignant about [their] methods of fighting"—and denounced Camus's "hollow" language.[40] Sartre was no less hostile. Less than a week after Camus's intervention in Algiers, Sartre spoke at a pro-FLN rally in Paris: taking clear aim at his former friend, he ridiculed "tender-hearted realists" who called for reforms in Algeria. The answer, Sartre declared, was revolution, not reform: "The neo-colonialist is a fool who still believes that the colonial system can be overhauled."[41]

Sartre, no doubt, also counted Germaine Tillion among the fools. Like Camus, she did not believe that the Arabs and Berbers were ready for independence; and like Camus, she mercilessly exposed the staggering economic and political hardships France had imposed on native Algerians. Her book, *L'Algérie en 1957*, introduced the notion of pauperization and created a firestorm of interest in France and abroad. Camus wrote the preface to the English-language translation: it was the only work on Algeria, he stated, that did not leave him with a "sense of unreality, unease, or anger."[42]

Like Camus, Tillion tried to patch together a truce. Nearly two years after Camus returned empty-handed to Paris, Tillion met with two of the senior leaders of the FLN, Yacef Saadi and Ali la Pointe. Impressed by Tillion's objectivity and her rigorous analysis, and worried by the successes notched up by the French military in the Battle of Algiers, Saadi arranged a clandestine meeting with her in Algiers. Taken to an underground apartment in the Kasbah, Tillion promptly told the FLN leaders that Algeria was not yet ready for full independence. As Saadi and la Pointe looked at her in astonishment, a furious Tillion added: "You are assassins." Saadi agreed with her but insisted that the FLN had no choice. Given the disproportionate size and capacity of the enemy, the FLN had to pursue a strategy of terror. Like Camus, Tillion firmly rejected this claim: one must always choose *not* to kill innocent people, she replied. Her reply persuaded the two men: they agreed to halt the FLN's killing of civilians while Tillion tried to persuade the French authorities to stop the executions of captured FLN fighters. It was, in effect, a civil truce—one remarkably close to Camus's own idea. The FLN kept its end of the bargain for several days, but the French military command continued to guillotine prisoners, sabotaging Tillion's efforts.[43]

Camus learned of Tillion's initiatives directly from her. In October 1957, she visited him in Paris and told him of her meeting with the FLN leaders. She also brought along the essays of Muslim grade school students. Their teacher had asked them to write on the question: "What would you do if you were invisible?" In every one of the essays, the student explored how he or she would devote his or her time to killing the French. Upon concluding his account in his journal, Camus wrote: "I despair for the future."[44]

o o o

By the time Tillion paid her visit, Camus was in the twentieth month of a self-imposed public silence on the subject of Algeria. In fact, only two days after Mollet's disastrous visit to Algiers, Camus resigned from *L'Express* and told his friends he would no longer speak or write on the torment of his native country. Mendès's defeat by the parliamentary system and Mollet's capitulation to the *pied noir* mob had smothered Camus's hope that the republic would prove equal to its ideals. Events had also demolished Camus's earlier conviction that neither *pied noir* nor Arab truly wanted to finish this race toward mutual destruction: as the Battle of Algiers soon revealed, each side was determined to pound the other into submission. What more could he say at this point? Nothing, he believed: silence was all he had left.

The clamor created by Camus's silence was deafening. Many on the Left were struck by the dissonance between Camus's responses to the USSR's invasion of Hungary in 1956 on the one hand and to France's increasing use of torture in Algeria on the other. When Soviet tanks lumbered into Budapest, Camus led the list of Western intellectuals to whom the rebels appealed. He replied immediately: he would never abandon "the October insurgents as long as liberty is not given back to the Hungarian people."[45]

While images of shattered barricades in Budapest flashed across the world, however, Algiers was the arena for a different form of urban warfare. The Battle of Algiers was under way, and the French military had institutionalized the use of torture. Reports grew so frequent that Beauvoir bitterly noted the "same boring program of electric goads, immersions, hangings, burnings, rape funnels, stakes, nails torn out, bones broken." As for her estranged friend Camus, Beauvoir "was revolted by [his] refusal to speak."[46] Even fellow *pieds noirs* such as Jean Daniel and Jules Roy had reluctantly come to accept the inevitability of Algerian independence and wondered over Camus's muteness. As his sense of separation deepened, Camus blamed it on his insistence to *parler vrai:* "If I have always refused to lie...it is because I could never accept solitude. But solitude should now also be accepted."[47]

The references to silence and solitude did not mean that Camus had joined the Trappists. In private he continued to talk about this "personal tragedy" with close friends.[48] More important, even if he did not speak publicly, he continued to act privately. He wrote more than 150 appeals for Arab prisoners facing imprisonment or death, sending his letters to government ministers or friends in the administration.[49] He pleaded for the lives of FLN militants as well as Communists, taking care in each case to note the specific circumstances: this prisoner did not kill blindly; that prisoner did not kill anyone at all. The appeals sometimes succeeded but more often failed, leaving Camus with a new appreciation for the absurd. A few days after sending a letter to President Coty asking him to pardon several militants, he read in the newspaper that three of the condemned men had been shot. *"Fifteen days after the execution,"* he observed, the president's aide "informs me that my letter held the attention of the President and was transmitted to the higher council of the magistracy. Bureaucracy of dreamers."[50]

∘ ∘ ∘

A different kind of bureaucracy of dreamers eventually forced Camus out of his stubbornly held silence. Two weeks after Tillion's visit in 1957, Camus was dining in a Paris restaurant when a waiter hurried to his table: the radio had just announced that Camus had won the Nobel Prize for Literature. On hearing the news, Camus grew pale and agitated: Malraux, he insisted, should have received the prize. The following day, he wrote in his journal: "Nobel. Strange feeling of overwhelming pressure and melancholy. At 20 years old, poor and naked, I knew true glory. My mother."[51]

It was natural that Camus should be burdened by the news. He suspected that politics had influenced the Swedish Academy: the Battle of Algiers had captured the world's attention and Camus represented the last, best chance for reconciliation. Did not the academy affirm that Camus's work "illuminated the problems of human conscience in our times"? The dilemma was that by breaking his silence, Camus would betray his conscience; by maintaining it, he would betray the world's expectations. No less troubling, just as he had nothing more to say on Algeria as an intellectual, Camus worried he had nothing more to offer the world as an artist. Apart from a collection of short stories, Camus had not published a work of fiction since *The Plague.* Tellingly, many other writers and critics in Paris agreed with Camus that Malraux should have been given the prize. "No matter what," he reminded himself, "I must overcome this sort of fear, of incomprehensible panic where this unexpected news has thrown me."[52]

When Camus arrived in Stockholm two months later to accept the prize, his fears were partly confirmed. A local newspaper welcomed his arrival with the question on most people's minds: Why was the conscience of his generation silent on his native Algeria? Swedish and foreign journalists did not press Camus for a direct reply. But Camus's circumspection gave way when, shortly before his official discourse, he met with a large gathering of university students in Stockholm. Few students asked about literature; instead, current events were on their minds, and the dialogue quickly veered toward Algeria. A Muslim student rose from the audience and demanded to know why Camus spoke so freely about violence in Eastern Europe but not in Algeria. Before Camus could reply, the student began to insult him. Waiting with scarcely controlled anger for the student to pause, Camus finally spoke: "I have never spoken to an Arab or to one of your militants as you have just spoken to me in public. You are for democracy in Algeria, so be democratic right now and let me speak."[53]

The student refused him this right, instead tossing new salvos of insults apparently supplied by a knot of students at the back of the room to whom he kept returning. One spectator had the "painful impression of an attack dog ordered to leap at [Camus's] throat."[54] It was as if everything and nothing had changed since his public lecture nearly two years before at the Cercle du Progrès: instead of enraged *pieds noirs*, it was now a representative of Muslim Algeria who refused to listen. Yet Camus insisted on being heard: "Though I have been silent for a year and eight months, that doesn't mean I have stopped acting. I've always been a supporter for a just Algeria in which two equal peoples would live peacefully. I've repeatedly demanded that justice be rendered to the Algerian people and that they be given full democratic rights." He had stopped speaking out for these rights because "the hatred on both sides is now so great that an intellectual can no longer intervene without taking the risk of making the violence worse." And so, Camus declared, he decided to wait for a moment when he could unite rather than divide peoples. As his frustration continued to mount, he told his antagonist that some of his comrades were "alive today thanks to efforts you are not aware of." He then turned to the heart of the matter, terror and his own family: "I have always condemned terror. But I must also condemn terrorism that strikes blindly, for example in the streets of Algiers, and which might strike my mother and family. I believe in justice, but I'll defend my mother before justice."[55]

o o o

When the conference ended, the battle over the meaning of Camus's celebrated declaration began. While the audience at Stockholm applauded on hearing it, the Left in Paris condemned it on reading the report in the next day's *Le Monde*. When the newspaper's cerebral editor, Hubert Beuve-Méry, first read his correspondent's account, he rubbed his eyes and demanded reconfirmation. When his reporter confirmed the quotation, Beuve-Méry muttered: "I knew Camus would say something bloody stupid."[56] As for Beauvoir, she thought that Camus had come clean: he was little more than a shill for the *pieds noirs:* "The fraud lay in the fact that he posed at the same time as a man above the battle, thus providing a warning for those who wanted to reconcile this war and its methods with bourgeois humanism."[57]

Michael Walzer has taken this critique and set it on its head: Camus does put the *pieds noirs* first but he is ethically justified in doing so. Objectivity, Walzer suggests, is not all it is cracked up to be: the "critical distance" of critics like Beauvoir and Sartre reduces the robustness of life, making for an "ideologically flattened world." Complexity and ambiguity, shadows and blur are all eliminated; vast canvases are turned into cartoons; political choices are made easy at the expense of different, often antagonistic truths.

Herein lies Camus's importance as an observer, Walzer argues. It is because of, not despite, his deep roots in Algeria that Camus's words and silences are so terribly important. Were it not for his particular identity, Camus would have lacked credibility with his fellow *pieds noirs;* were it not for his particular experiences, he would have lacked clarity on the tragic implications of the war. Camus believed the "values I ought to defend and illustrate today are average values. This requires a talent so spare and unadorned that I doubt I have it."[58] These everyday values were the universal claims of French republicanism refracted through the sights and sounds of Belcourt. While the process of refraction takes in both the *pieds noirs* and the Arabs, it focuses most particularly on *les siens:* one's own community. "Camus would not have said...that French and Arab lives were of equal importance in his eyes." This is as it should be, Walzer reassures us: "Morality required the mutual acceptance, not the abolition or transcendence, of these different meanings. The Frenchmen had his own loyalties, and so did the Arab; and each had a right to his own."[59]

This claim is intriguing but also questionable. Walzer's interpretation may have been the perspective of Raymond, or even of Meursault, in *The Stranger*, but it was not Camus's perspective. Had he been truly incapable of taking the distance required to measure the claims of both sides, Camus would not have become silent—or, at least, not in the same way. From his youthful days as a militant in the PCF and a reporter for *Alger-Républicain* to his mature days as editor of *Combat* and advocate of a civil truce, Camus represented Arabs and Berbers no less than the European working class of Belcourt. If, as Walzer writes, Camus's silence was "eloquent in its hopelessness," it is not because he refused to surrender his primal loyalties to the *pied noir* community. Instead, Camus refused to surrender his loyalty to *both* communities, just as he would not surrender his lucidity in regard to the tragic character of the human condition.[60]

Apart from one other instance—the introduction he wrote for *Actuelles III*, a collection of editorials and letters on the subject of Algeria—Camus never again spoke publicly about his native country's torment.[61] We, on the other hand, still mine his silence for meaning. Much has been said about it, all of it nonsensical. This is inevitable and will inevitably continue: silence invites interpretation, but the moment interpretation begins, it undercuts the fundamental character of silence.

But it is no less necessary to keep on with the nonsense. This, at least, was the view of the "other North African," Augustine. Early in his *Confessions*, Augustine wonders about God's nature, while acknowledging the fundamental insufficiency of any human answer. What else would one expect, given the limits of language on the one hand and God's utter lack of limits on the other? Augustine embraces this paradox: "What has anyone achieved in words when he speaks about you? Yet woe to those who are silent about you because, though loquacious with verbosity, they have nothing to say."[62]

So, too, does Ludwig Wittgenstein. Measured by climate or culture, few cities in the twentieth century were further from Algiers than Vienna. No less distant from each other were the lives and work of Wittgenstein and Camus. Each of the two men, moreover, seems to have been utterly unaware of or indifferent to the other's work.[63] And yet they had a common love for Augustine: the Viennese thinker believed the *Confessions* to be the "most serious book every written" and was especially drawn to Augustine's preoccupation with getting language right. In this spirit, Wittgenstein translated Augustine's puzzling exhortation in book I as follows: "And woe to those who say nothing concerning thee just because the chatterboxes talk a lot of nonsense."[64]

Camus and Wittgenstein also shared a concern for getting both words and actions right—a concern so deep that, at times, it debilitated both men. Ethics and language, they agreed, were closely connected; to act well meant to speak well; and silence, in an important though elusive sense, was an essential aspect of the relationship between saying and acting. Perhaps the most famous line of twentieth-century philosophy is the last sentence in Wittgenstein's first book, the *Tractatus Logico-Philosophicus,* completed at the end of the same war that, at its start, left the infant Camus fatherless: "Whereof one cannot speak, thereof one must be silent."

As one commentator notes, this observation contains both a logical truth and an ethical command.[65] We must always strive to articulate meaning, yet we will always be foiled by the limitations of language. It is hardly true, however, that what falls outside the realm of the "sayable" does not exist. As Wittgenstein warned, it is simply "unsayable." But, he added, it can be *shown* through traditional metaphysical claims or, to be sure, through the refusal to articulate any claim at all. After all, Wittgenstein described the *Tractatus* as a ladder to be thrown away once we attain our goal—a goal where language is no longer required.

In the only "popular" lecture he ever gave, Wittgenstein spoke on ethics. As his *Tractatus* shows, any attempt to formulate an ethics inevitably leads to nonsense, but this must not prevent us from continuing our efforts: "This running against the walls of our [linguistic] cage is perfectly, absolutely hopeless. Ethics so far as it springs from the desire to say something about the meaning of life, the absolute good, the absolute valuable, can be no science. What it says does not add to our knowledge in any sense. But it is a document of a tendency in the human mind which I personally cannot help respecting deeply and I would not for my life ridicule it."[66]

These sentiments mirror Camus's attitude toward Christianity. But, more important, they suggest a new meaning to his final silence. In 1953, two years before the tragedies of Philippeville, Camus published "Return to Tipasa." In this essay on his native Algeria, he tried to balance the two great forces in his life "even when they contradict one another": the wonder of the world and the equally sublime ethical duties of the individual. "Yes, there is beauty and there are the humiliated. Whatever difficulties the enterprise may present, I would like never to be unfaithful either to one or the other." But, he continues, "this still sounds like ethics, and we live for something that transcends ethics. If we could name it, what silence would follow!"[67]

Camus's silence does not transcend ethics but instead reflects an ethics similar to Wittgenstein's. Tony Judt is right to suggest that Camus's silence was an "extension of his earlier promise to speak out for the truth," but wrong to conclude that in the "Algerian case there was no longer any truth, just feelings."[68] On the contrary, there were truths, but tragically, they were incompatible with the feelings. For Camus, Algeria was not an abstraction but rather his very life. It was, in part, precisely because he *was* a *pied noir* that Camus was ideally placed to express the Algerian dilemma. In a letter Camus sent to *Le Monde* shortly after his trip to Stockholm, he wrote that he felt closer to the Muslim student at the meeting than those "Frenchmen who talk about Algeria without knowing it." His young antagonist, at least, "knew what he was talking about." His face, Camus added, was not marked by hatred, but by "despair and unhappiness. I share that unhappiness: his is the face of my country."[69]

A detached or "objective" critic, like a rooted or "subjective" critic, is perfectly capable of silence. But such a critic makes a different sound of silence. The muteness of the "objective" observer may well signal indifference, while, as Walzer notes, "the silence of the connected social critic is a grim sign—a sign of defeat, a sign of endings."[70] This was certainly the case for Camus. In his Nobel lecture—given two days after his encounter with the Algerian student—Camus said that silence, at times, "takes on a terrifying sense."[71] The Algerian conflict was, for Camus, one of those moments. Euripides impressed Camus much less than Aeschylus and Sophocles: unlike his predecessors, the author of *Medea* failed to depict the "pessimistic and tragic Greece" he felt to be truest.[72] To be sure, Euripides had a weakness for the deus ex machina that would lift his protagonists from an otherwise paralyzing knot of equally powerful but opposing claims. For Algeria, Camus ultimately understood, there could be no deus ex machina.

EPILOGUE

In the same way as a writer's death makes us exaggerate
the importance of his work, a person's death makes us exaggerate
the importance of his place among us. Thus the past is wholly
made up of death, which peoples it with illusions.

In the same year that Camus won the Nobel Prize and briefly broke his silence over Algeria, he published a short story called "The Guest." The tale is one of the few explicitly situated in the midst of the Algerian conflict. A powerful snowstorm has blanketed a harsh region of Algeria where a *pied noir* named Daru works as a grade school teacher. Soon after the storm lifts, he receives a visit from Balducci, a gendarme with whom he is on good terms. Mounted on a horse that slowly climbs the slope to the school, Balducci leads an Arab, who is on foot and tied to a rope. Once Balducci reaches Daru, he tells him that his unnamed prisoner is to be tried for the murder of a fellow Arab.

Daru then learns the reason for Balducci's visit: he has been ordered by the authorities to turn the prisoner over to Daru, who in turn is to take him to the local administrative seat in Tinguit. Dismayed by the message, Daru protests that he will not obey the orders. Despite Balducci's repeated efforts, the teacher insists that, while disgusted by the man's crime, he will not turn him in. Balducci finally shrugs his shoulders. Turning the prisoner over to Daru, he tells him to do what he sees fit: "If you want to break with us, go ahead, I won't denounce you. I have orders to hand over the prisoner: I'm doing it."[1] He places his revolver on Daru's desk and leaves.

Alone with the prisoner, whose hands had been untied at Daru's request, the teacher puts the gun in his pocket and goes into his own room, which adjoins the school. Lying on his couch, he stares out the window, "watching the sky gradually close over, listening to the silence. It was this silence that had seemed difficult to him in the first days after his arrival."[2] Yet, though the "solitude and silence had been hard for him in these merciless lands inhabited only by stones," Daru had grown accustomed to them. This world, he reflects, was "a cruel place to live, even without the men.... And yet outside this desert, neither of them, Daru knew, could have truly lived."[3]

Nor, it appears, can Daru and his guest live together for very long, even in the desert. As night descends, the two men exchange barely a dozen words. Much to the Arab's astonishment, Daru shares with him a simple dinner. He asks Daru why he is eating with him, to which the teacher replies: "I'm hungry."[4] They also share a room to bunk down for the night. After Daru has made the beds, there is nothing more to do—except, that is, try to connect. Daru "had to take a look at this man."[5] When Daru asks the Arab why he killed the man, he replies obliquely: "He was running away. I ran after him." To Daru's second question— "Are you sorry?"—the uncomprehending Arab has no answer. But equally inadequate is Daru's answer to the Arab's insistent question about what will happen to him next: "I don't know," he says twice.[6]

Eventually, the two men fall asleep in the small stove-heated room. At one point, the Arab stirs, rises from his bed, and steps outside. Awakened by the opening of the latch, Daru watches the dark shape slip through the door; with relief, he thinks the Arab is running away. He then hears the sound of running water and, a few minutes later, sees the door reopen: the Arab slides back in and returns to his bed.

The next morning, making coffee for himself and his uninvited guest, Daru silently curses "both his own people, who had sent him this Arab, and the man himself who had dared to kill and hadn't known enough to run away." He prepares a satchel of food, dons his jacket, and leads the Arab outside, locking the school door behind him. The two men walk for hours across the snow-clad landscape, finally reaching the edge of the plateau. Daru turns to the Arab, hands him the food satchel, and points east. If you go that way, the Frenchman tells the Arab, you will reach Tinguit, where the police are waiting. Daru then motions toward the south and says: "A day's walk from here you'll find pastures and the first nomads. They will welcome you and give you shelter, according to their law."[7]

Daru turns around and returns to his school. On reaching a nearby hilltop, however, he stops to look back at the plain. He sees, "his heart aching, the Arab slowly making his way along the road to the prison."[8] The story ends one paragraph later with Daru back in his school, again staring out the window at the sky. On the wall behind him hangs a blackboard; when school was still in session Daru had drawn on it the courses of the principal French rivers. But now, imposed over this map was a clumsily written message: "You turned in our brother. You will pay."[9]

o o o

In scarcely twenty pages, written during the last period of his life, Camus returned to his "few familiar ideas." Against an austere Algerian landscape, "The Guest" depicts the clash between the obligations of justice and liberty. At one level, the tension between the two imperatives is straightforward: the Arab is accused of a crime, Daru is charged with bringing him to justice; the Arab is a prisoner, Daru sets him free. But the plainness of the prose and the severity of the scenery conjure a mirage of sorts: the clipped language and bare land eventually dissolve into blurred and elusive lines of motivation and action. While Daru knows that the Arab killed another man, he does not know the precise nature of the crime. His effort to cast light on the event sputters and fails when the Arab avoids his questions. We never grasp what the Arab did, just as we never plumb the Arab's mind. Expressing the story's harsh epistemology is Balducci's reply when Daru asks if the Arab is "against us": "I don't think so. But you never know."[10] Nor, for that matter, do we fully understand Daru. At the climax of his disagreement with Balducci, the teacher exclaims: "All of this disgusts me, and your boy first and foremost. But I won't turn him in. Fight for myself, yes, if need be. But not that."[11] But the adjectival pronouns are unmoored: to what, precisely, does "that" refer? The brewing war? The ostensible crime? The role Daru is ordered to play? In the end, Daru never clearly states what disgusts him; nor does he say what he will *not* fight for.

What is clear is that Daru is a loner, different from the society he has fled; as Balducci tells him, "You've always been a little crazy."[12] Equally clear is that he conceives of justice in a broader manner, as an impersonal weight, a view the ancient Greeks would have readily recognized. More than once, Daru reflects on the immense forces at work in nature—forces to which men and their doings must sooner or later bend and submit. Even before the arrival of his guest, he had come to understand life's cycle: "Towns sprang up, flourished, then disappeared; men passed through, loved each other or cut each other's throats, then died."[13] The rise and fall of cities, the birth and death of generations, all under an impassive sky and unblinking sun: these massive and ageless scales, slowly tilting one way, then the other, constitute justice.

But this sublime structure does not free man of responsibility; on the contrary, it impels him to seek purely human forms of justice. Attending to others is one expression of this task. Sitting across from the Arab, Daru "had to take a look at this man." He studies his "guest," refusing to see him as an abstraction. In one sense, Daru fails in his effort: he sees nothing "but the dark, shining eyes, and the animal mouth." But he does not give up. Rather than seeing the Arab as a pawn in an unspoken war or an object of impersonal justice, Daru insists on his dignity and autonomy. This nameless guest must, like Daru, act on his own. The Arab's choice—to take the road to Tinguit, where prison or worse awaits—is a source of despair, but how much greater Daru's despair would have been if he had led him there himself.

A corollary to this conception of human justice is our need to see the world clearly. Or, since we can never see it with complete clarity, to at least view it with what Iris Murdoch calls "increasing precision." The improvement of our moral being, according to Murdoch, follows from the improvement of our vision: it turns us away from ourselves and toward others and the world. Daru does not speak in abstractions or grand phrases. In fact, he speaks rarely; when he does speak, he is terse. His language is as arid as the landscape; he can no more be separated from one than from the other: "Anywhere else, he felt exiled." While Daru might have an unrealistic sense of what he can do—Balducci laughs when Daru tells him he can defend himself with an old hunting rifle—he nevertheless has fewer illusions than most people have about the world. He remains faithful both to the world and to its inhabitants: he sees his fellow men with the same exactitude and precision with which he observes the rocks and ridges of his physical world.

The story leaves Daru standing at the classroom window as the sun resumes its daily assault on the world. Back turned to the ominous message inscribed on the board, he looks north toward the sea: "He watched distractedly as the yellow light leaped from the heights of the sky and spread across the whole surface of the plateau." The last line—"In this vast country he had loved so much, he was alone"—rings with the finality of an epitaph. Yet finality, at least in terms of our comprehension, is never achieved. Critics have noted the ambiguity of the story's title: the French word "hôte" can mean either "guest" or "host"—an etymological confusion that reflects Daru's own life. He is, of course, a host who welcomes Balducci and his prisoner to his home. Yet Daru discovers he is also a stranger in what he always believed to be his own land. He has spent his life feeling like an outsider anywhere but in Algeria but is now also exiled from his native land. An awful truth dawns on Daru: the historical, cultural, and linguistic division between the *pieds noirs* and the Arabs—both of whom are simultaneously hosts and guests to each other—is too great to bridge.

By the last years of his life, Camus had come up hard against this division. Hence his silence: What more could be said about events whose tragic dimensions beggared language? Camus's muteness spoke to his inability to deny the legitimate rights of either the *pied noir* or Arab communities. For Daru, this ethical lucidity estranges him from both Balducci and the Arabs. So, too, for Camus: his insistence on calling things by their names eventually forced him into silence. Both men are moralists and, consequently, both men are condemned to a life of exile.

But Daru's and Camus's common plight is, for want of a better word, also metaphysical. The relationship these men have to the universe is as uncertain as their relationship to Algeria. Are they guests? Or are they hosts? Being a host implies knowledge and duties, while being a guest entails rights and protections. But in this silent and indifferent world, both Daru and Camus seem no less deprived of a host's knowledge than of a guest's rights. This fundamental instability—this inability to know where one stands in relation to others and the world—is just another way of acknowledging our absurd condition.

Yet Daru does what he has to do: he refuses to close his eyes. His unblinking vision is such that when the moment comes to act, his choice has already been made. As Murdoch notes, freedom is "not the sudden jumping of the isolated will in and out of an impersonal logical complex, it is a function of the progressive attempt to see a particular object clearly."[14] Daru resists viewing the world through racial, political, or ideological prisms; instead, he sees only a world of particular and singular objects. This is not a matter of moral vision, as Murdoch observes, since there is nothing to see morally. "There is only the ordinary world which is seen with ordinary vision."[15]

As the story reveals, seeing the world clearly and making the right moral choices do not change the world. But this is not the point— no more the point, at least, than Sisyphus trying to change the world by endlessly and repeatedly pushing the boulder up the slope. The importance of the act instead lies in "increasing perfection"—attending to the task at hand, in other words, and getting it "more" right. But unlike Sisyphus's task, Daru's work does not occur on a desolate mountainside. Or rather, it does occur in such a place, but Daru, unlike Sisyphus, is not alone. A fellow man appears whose anonymity, rather than making him an inhuman figure, instead makes him fully human. Daru seemingly fails in his effort to liberate this man; in fact, his action brings catastrophe down on his own head. Yet he does not regret what he has done. Just as we must imagine Sisyphus happy, so too must we imagine Daru, if not happy, at least at peace with the choice he has made.

o o o

Soon after the completion of "The Guest," Camus observed in his journals: "In the Old Testament God says nothing, it is the living people who serve him with their words. It is because of this that I have not stopped loving that which is sacred in this world."[16] For Camus, service to others is as sacred as anything can be in a world shorn of transcendental meaning. Service is worthy of respect and veneration even—or especially—in the face of silence and is based on the fundamental recognition that the other is equally implicated and enmeshed in an absurd world. Among the ways we serve is through communication: because of the silence hanging over our lives, we must speak to and for ourselves, to and for others. We do so not only in the face of silence, but in order to give voice to that silence.

Probing silence is the task of the artist as well as the moralist. For most of his life, Camus dwelt on the changing nature of silence. He identified silence, like the state of childhood innocence, with his mother. Camus's silence later came to express the tragic reality of Algeria and the tragic reality of the human condition. And silence followed in the wake of attention. Simone Weil spoke to this idea when she asked about the true value of solitude: "For in solitude we are in the presence of mere matter...things of less value (perhaps) than a human spirit. Its value lies in the greater possibility of attention. If we could be attentive to the same degree in the presence of a human being."[17] True attention, for Camus as for Weil, requires the degree of concentration that we give to objects but rarely to human beings. We do not feel uneasy when we silently attend to a sweeping mountain range, a towering cathedral, or an achingly beautiful painting. The moment and setting quite naturally call on us to stop, fall silent, and see.

But we feel deeply uneasy attending with the same intensity to a fellow man or woman. Yet this should be no less natural than paying attention to the material world. Daru does this in his life, just as Camus did in his art: with unusual clarity and empathy he turned his attention to our lives. Through his work as a novelist, Camus created characters that excel at the work of seeing. From Meursault and Sisyphus to Rieux and Tarrou to Cormery and Daru, Camus gave voice to the often mute but always critical work of attention. Each of these characters embodies Camus's insistence that, "in the presence of the world, I have no wish to lie or to be lied to. I want to keep my lucidity to the last, and gaze upon my death with all the fullness of my jealousy and horror."[18]

Equally important, as a journalist and essayist Camus represented lives and situations that otherwise would have been condemned to silence. We always take a step forward when we discover a human problem behind the facade of a political problem, Camus insisted. But the human problem of course must first be made manifest. No matter how uneasy this task makes us—and Camus often admits to being *mal dans sa peau*—we must confront it. This imperative, for Camus, applies to political injustice and to social inequities. In our age, he warned in his Nobel speech, artists must assume their responsibilities toward their fellow men and women.

In his stubborn commitment to the world of politics, Camus understood better than anyone else that existential despair was a luxury the poor and oppressed could not afford. But he also understood that his responsibilities as an artist went beyond the realm of politics. In a world that denies us transcendental solace, the artist's task is to justify the pursuit of meaning by human beings. At the heart of Camus's writing, as Jeffrey Isaac notes, is "a conception of humans as agents who, as possessors of interpretative and material powers, seek to sustain value in their world."[19] We are overmatched and inevitably overwhelmed in this struggle, but this is not cause for despair. As the work of Camus will always serve to remind us, true despair occurs only when "we no longer know the reasons for struggling, or if it is even necessary to struggle."[20] Like Jacques Cormery gazing at his father's tombstone, most of us have already, or will one day soon, reach the age when we realize with a shock that we are older than Camus, but that the reasons for struggling are ageless.

NOTES

Regarding Camus

1. Albert Camus, "The Wind at Djemila," in *Lyrical and Critical Essays*, trans. Ellen Kennedy (New York: Knopf, 1968), 76.

2. Siân Miles, ed., *Simone Weil: An Anthology* (New York: Weidenfeld and Nicolson, 1986), 5.

3. Quoted in Olivier Todd, *Albert Camus: Une vie* (Paris: Gallimard, 1996), 593. Throughout this book, passages quoted from the French are my translation, unless an English-language source is cited in the notes.

4. Albert Camus, *Discours de Suède* (Paris: Gallimard, 1958), 17.

5. Albert Camus, *Fragments d'un combat: 1938–1940*, vol. 2, ed. Jacqueline Lévi-Valensi (Paris: Gallimard, 1978), 720.

6. Ibid., 730.

7. See the chapter on Camus in Tony Judt, *The Burden of Responsibility* (Chicago: University of Chicago Press, 1998), 87–135.

8. Albert Camus, *The Myth of Sisyphus and Other Essays*, trans. Justin O'Brien (New York: Vintage, 1991), 21.

9. Quoted in John Foley, *Albert Camus: From the Absurd to Revolt* (Montreal: McGill-Queen's University Press, 2008), 4.

10. Albert Camus, *The First Man*, trans. David Hapgood (New York: Knopf, 1995), 25.

11. "Lettre à Jean de Maisonseul," in Albert Camus, *Oeuvres complètes*, vol. I, ed. Jacqueline Lévi-Valensi (Paris: Gallimard: 2006), 97.

12. Preface to Camus, *Lyrical and Critical Essays*, 5–6.

13. Camus, *The First Man*, 41.

14. Albert Camus, "Between Yes and No," in *Lyrical and Critical Essays*, 32.

15. Quoted in Alba Amoia, "Sun, Sea and Geraniums: Camus en voyage," in *Critical Essays on Albert Camus*, ed. Bettina Knapp (Boston: G.K. Hall: 1988), 67.

16. Albert Camus, "Nuptials at Tipasa," in *Lyrical and Critical Essays*, 68.

17. Camus, *The First Man*, 146.

18. Camus, "Between Yes and No," 32.

19. Camus, *The First Man*, 98.

20. Camus, "Between Yes and No," 37.

21. Albert Camus, *Notebooks 1951–1959*, trans. Ryan Bloom (Chicago: Ivan Dee, 2008), 125.

22. Camus, "Between Yes and No," 33–34.

23. Ibid., 35–36.

24. Albert Camus, "The Enigma," in *Lyrical and Critical Essays*, 161.

25. Albert Camus, "Return to Tipasa," in *Lyrical and Critical Essays*, 167–168.

26. Ibid., 169–170.

27. Camus, *The First Man*, 96.

28. Albert Camus, "Preface to The Wrong and the Right Side," in *Lyrical and Critical Essays*, 16.

29. Quoted in Ray Monk, *Ludwig Wittgenstein: The Duty of Genius* (New York: Free Press, 1990), 277.

1939: From County Mayo to Kabylia

Epigraph. "Return to Tipasa," in *Lyrical and Critical Essays*, trans. Ellen Kennedy (New York: Knopf, 1968), 169–170.

1. Albert Camus, *Notebooks 1935–1951*, trans. Philip Thody (New York: Marlowe, 1998), 60. This Marlowe edition combines two different notebooks, which were originally published separately: *Notebooks 1935–1942*, trans. Philip Thody, and *Notebooks 1942–1951*, trans. Justin O'Brien. The original pagination for each notebook is retained (i.e., the first page of *Notebooks 1942–1951* starts again with page I). Hereafter, if the source is this Marlowe edition I will cite either Camus, *Notebooks 1935–1942*, trans. Thody, or *Notebooks 1942–1951*, trans. O'Brien.

2. Albert Camus, quoted in Mark Orme, *The Development of Albert Camus's Concern for Social and Political Justice* (Madison, N.J.: Fairleigh Dickinson University Press, 2007), 37.

3. Albert Camus, *Discours de Suède* (Paris: Gallimard, 1958), 17.

4. Olivier Todd, *Albert Camus: Une vie* (Paris: Gallimard, 1996), 120.

5. Quoted in Christine Margerrison, "Camus and the Theater," in *The Cambridge Companion to Camus*, ed. Edward J. Hughes (Cambridge: Cambridge University Press, 2007), 69.

6. Todd, *Une vie*, 121; Roger Quilliot, quoted in Neil Oxenhandler, *Looking for Heroes in Postwar France* (Dartmouth: University of New England Press, 1996), 49–50.

7. Albert Camus, "La mer au plus près," *Oeuvres complètes*, vol. 2, ed. Jecqueline Lévi-Valensi (Paris: Gallimard, 2006), 879; Camus, *Notebooks 1935–1942*, trans. Thody, 173.

8. Ibid., 37, 106.

9. Ibid., 64.

10. Ibid., 15.

11. Patrick McCarthy, *Camus* (New York: Random House, 1982), 84.

12. Albert Camus, *The Rebel*, trans. Anthony Bower (New York: Vintage, 1992), 284.

13. Quoted in Orme, *Development of Camus's Concern* (Madison: Fairleigh Dickinson University Press, 2007), 59.

14. Jacqueline Lévi-Valensi and André Abbou, eds., *Cahiers Albert Camus 3: Fragments d'un combat*, vol. 2 (Paris: Gallimard 1978), 677.

15. Camus, *Oeuvres complètes*, 2:1800.

16. Herbert Lottman, *Albert Camus* (Corte Madera: Gingko Press, 1997), 47.

17. Albert Camus, *Essais*, ed. Roger Quilliot (Paris: Gallimard, 1965), 1216–1217.

18. See Todd, *Une vie*, 128.

19. Camus, *Correspondence*, 111.

20. Jean Grenier, quoted in Toby Garfitt, "Situating Camus: The Formative Influences," in Hugues, *The Cambridge Companion to Camus*, 34.

21. Camus, *Notebooks 1935–1942*, trans. Thody, 28.

22. For an account of this obscure engagement, see Lottman, *Albert Camus*, 59.

23. Alice Conklin argues that, if "the empire endured as long as it did, it was in part because French racism often worked hand-in-hand with more progressive values." See *A Mission to Civilize* (Palo Alto: Stanford University Press, 1997), 256. See also Todd Shephard, *The Invention of Decolonization* (Ithaca: Cornell University Press, 2006), which depicts the conflict between official French policy in Algeria, founded on republican and egalitarian principles, and the racism exhibited by the local bureaucracy.

24. Camus, *Oeuvres complètes*, vol. 1, ed. Jacqueline Lévi-Valensi (Paris: Gallimard: 2006), 57.

25. Quoted in Todd, *Une vie*, 90.

26. I believe Paul Archambault is right to suggest that it "could be that nothing in Camus would have been different had he never heard of Augustine; but I am inclined to think that Augustine served as a mirror that allowed Camus to discover those qualities that became characteristically his." See his *Camus' Hellenic Sources* (Chapel Hill: University of North Carolina Press, 1971), 167.

27. Camus, *Oeuvres complètes*, 1:854.

28. Lévi-Valensi and Abbou, *Fragments d'un combat*, 1:58.

29. Quoted in Todd, *Une vie*, 179.

30. Lévi-Valensi and Abbou, *Fragments d'un combat*, 2:362.

31. Camus, *Notebooks 1935–1942*, trans. Thody, 24.

32. Lévi-Valensi and Abbou, *Fragments d'un combat*, 2:368.

33. Ibid., 513.

34. Ibid., 523.

35. Ibid., 529.

36. Ibid., 528.

37. Albert Camus, "Preface to The Wrong Side and the Right Side," in *Lyrical and Critical Essays*, trans. Ellen Kennedy (New York: Knopf, 1968), 8.

38. Quoted in John Ruedy, *Modern Algeria: The Origins and Development of a Nation* (Bloomington: Indiana University Press, 1992), 79. My historical account of Kabylia is indebted to Ruedy's monograph.

39. Lévi-Valensi and Abbou, *Fragments d'un combat*, 1:278–279.

40. Jacques Copeau, *Appels* (Paris: Gallimard, 1974), 223.

41. Lévi-Valensi and Abbou, *Fragments d'un combat*, 1:279.

42. See Camus, *Notebooks 1935–1942*, trans. Thody, 71.

43. Lévi-Valensi and Abbou, *Fragments d'un combat*, 1:288. The reference to Berber companions is in McCarthy, *Camus*, 118.

44. Lévi-Valensi and Abbou, *Fragments d'un combat*, 1:283.

45. Albert Camus, "The New Mediterranean Culture," in *Lyrical and Critical Essays*, 194.

46. Albert Camus, "Summer in Algiers," in *Lyrical and Critical Essays*, 90.

47. Lévi-Valensi and Abbou, *Fragments d'un combat*, 1:281.

48. Ibid., 289.

49. Ibid., 288.

50. Ibid., 314.

51. Ibid., 314.

52. Ibid., 335–336.

53. Ibid., 300.

54. Michel Walzer, *The Company of Critics* (New York: Basic Books, 1988), 68.

55. Lévi-Valensi and Abbou, *Fragments d'un combat*, 1:335.

56. Ibid., 274.

57. Ibid., 275.

58. Lévi-Valensi and Abbou, *Fragments d'un combat,* 2:531.

59. Quoted in Lottman, *Albert Camus,* 226.

60. Lévi-Valensi and Abbou, *Fragments d'un combat,* 2:695.

61. Ibid., 691–692.

62. Quoted in Lottman, *Albert Camus,* 224.

63. Lévi-Valensi and Abbou, *Fragments d'un combat,* 2:733.

64. Ibid., 736.

65. Tony Judt, *The Burden of Responsibility* (Chicago: University of Chicago Press, 1998), 122.

66. Quoted in Nicholas Grene, *Synge: A Critical Study of the Plays* (London: Macmillan, 1975), I.

67. Albert Camus, "Return to Tipasa," in *Lyrical and Critical Essays,* 169.

1945: A Moralist on the Barricades

Epigraph. Albert Camus, *Notebooks 1942–1951,* trans. Justin O'Brien (New York: Marlowe, 1998), 182.

1. Quoted in Colin Jones, *Paris: The Biography of a City* (New York: Viking, 2004), 427. For a survey of the desperate material conditions in Paris, see Dominique Veillon, *Vivre et survivre en France: 1939–1947* (Paris: Payot, 2004).

2. Albert Camus, *Between Hell and Reason,* trans. Alexandre de Gramont (Wesleyan University Press, 1991), 43.

3. Ibid., 39–40; Albert Camus, *Essais,* ed. Roger Quilliot (Paris: Gallimard, 1965), 1520.

4. Camus, *Notebooks 1942–1951,* trans. O'Brien, 24.

5. Ibid., 26.

6. Herbert Lottman, *Albert Camus* (Corte Madera: Gingko Press, 1997), 264.

7. Albert Camus, *Notebooks 1935–1942,* trans. Philip Thody (New York: Marlowe, 1998), 103.

8. Albert Camus, *The Stranger,* trans. Matthew Ward (New York: Vintage, 1989), 41.

9. Ibid., 59.

10. Ibid., 50.

11. Ibid., 66.

12. Ibid., 69.

13. Conor Cruise O'Brien, *Albert Camus of Europe and Africa* (New York: Viking, 1970), 25–26.

14. See David Carroll, *Albert Camus the Algerian* (New York: Columbia University Press, 2007), in particular chap. I.

15. Quoted in Olivier Todd, *Albert Camus: Une vie* (Paris: Gallimard, 1996), 256.

16. Quoted in Ibid., 257–258.

17. Carroll, *Albert Camus the Algerian*, 33.

18. Camus, *The Stranger*, 85.

19. Camus, *Notebooks 1942–1951*, trans. O'Brien, 42.

20. Ibid., 24.

21. The classic account of Le Chambon is Philip Haillie, *Lest Innocent Blood Be Shed* (New York: Harper and Row, 1979).

22. Haillie, *Lest Innocent Blood Be Shed*, 103.

23. Albert Camus, "Summer in Algiers," in *Lyrical and Critical Essays*, trans. Philip Thody (New York: Knopf, 1968), 90.

24. Camus, *Notebooks 1935–1942*, trans. Thody, 93.

25. Tony Judt, *Past Imperfect: French Intellectuals 1944–1956* (Berkeley: University of California Press, 1992), 61.

26. Albert Camus, "La profession de journaliste," in *Oeuvres complètes*, vol. I, ed. Jacqueline Lévi-Valensi (Paris: Gallimard, 2006), 920.

27. Camus, *Between Hell and Reason*, 45–46.

28. Todd, *Une vie*, 347.

29. Ibid., 327.

30. Albert Camus, *Lettres à un ami allemand* (Paris: Gallimard, 1948), 71–72.

31. Ibid., 78.

32. Quoted in David Carroll, *French Literary Fascism* (Princeton: Princeton University Press, 1995), 123.

33. Quoted in Alice Kaplan, *The Collaborator: The Trial and Execution of Robert Brasillach* (Chicago: University of Chicago Press, 2000), 49–50, 51, 58.

34. Quoted in Ibid., 172–173.

35. Quoted in Jean Lacouture, *François Mauriac* (Paris: Editions du Seuil, 1980), 389–390.

36. Quoted in Ibid., 408.

37. *Essais*, 1469.

38. Camus, *The Stranger*, 110.

39. Albert Camus, "Tout ne s'arrange pas," in *Oeuvres complètes*, 1:922.

40. In his *Arendt, Camus and Modern Rebellion* (New Haven: Yale University Press 1992), Jeffrey Isaac elaborates on this important parallel.

41. Camus, *Between Hell and Reason*, 42.

42. Ibid., 68.

43. Quoted in Jean Lacouture, *François Mauriac*, 412.

44. Camus, *Between Hell and Reason*, 72.

45. Ibid., 99.

46. Ibid., 102.

47. Quoted in Michel Winock, *Le siècle des intellectuels* (Paris: Seuil, 1997), 383.

48. Camus, *Between Hell and Reason*, 103–105.

49. Lottman, *Albert Camus*, 367–368.

50. Albert Camus, "Réflexions sur la guillotine," in *Essais*, 1021.

51. Quoted in Kaplan, *The Collaborator*, 198.

52. Camus, *Notebooks 1942–1951*, trans. O'Brien, 99.

53. Ibid., 99, my emphasis.

54. Ibid., 195.

55. Quoted in Kaplan, *The Collaborator*, 212. A short time after the execution, when his personal secretary told him he still regretted Brasillach's death, de Gaulle cut him short: "What of it? He was shot, like a soldier!" Quoted in Jean Lacouture, *De Gaulle: The Ruler 1945–1970*, trans. Alan Sheridan (New York: Norton, 1992), 81.

56. Quoted in Lacouture, *De Gaulle: The Ruler*, 79.

57. Camus, *Notebooks 1942–1951*, trans. O'Brien, 147.

58. Sébastien-Roch Nicolas Chamfort, *Maximes et anecdotes. Avec une biographie par Ginguené et une introduction par Albert Camus* (Monaco: DAC, 1944). Camus's introduction is reprinted in Sébastien-Roch Nicolas Chamfort, *Oeuvres complètes*, vol. I, ed. Jacqueline Lévi-Valensi (Paris: Gallimard, 2006), 923–933.

59. Albert Camus, introduction to Chamfort, *Maximes et anecdotes*, 924.

60. Ibid., 929.

61. Ibid., 932.

62. Iris Murdoch, *The Sovereignty of Good* (New York: Routledge, 2007), 46.

63. Ibid., 84–85.

64. Ibid., 52.

65. Murdoch, "The Existentialist Hero," in *Existentialists and Mystics*, ed., Peter Conradi (New York: Penguin, 1997), 114.

66. Camus, *Between Hell and Reason*, 112.

67. Camus, *Oeuvres complètes*, 2:471.

68. Ibid., 471.

1952: French Tragedies

Epigraph. Albert Camus, *Notebooks 1942–1951*, trans. Justin O'Brien (New York: Marlowe, 1998), 119.

1. Albert Camus, *Notebooks 1951–1959*, trans. Ryan Bloom (Chicago: Ivan Dee, 2008), 20.

2. See Herbert Lottman, *Albert Camus* (Corte Madera: Gingko Press, 1997), 522–523.

3. Tony Judt, *Past Imperfect: French Intellectuals 1944–1956* (Berkeley: University of California Press, 1992), 119.

4. Simone de Beauvoir, *Force of Circumstance,* trans. Richard Howard (New York: Penguin, 1963), 264.

5. Simone de Beauvoir, *La force de l'âge* (Paris: Gallimard, 1960), 616–617.

6. Albert Camus, "The Enigma," in *Lyrical and Critical Essays,* trans. Philip Thody (New York: Knopf, 1968), 160.

7. As Paul Archambault notes, this exchange does not appear in Aeschylus's tragedy but was instead invented by Camus. See his *Camus' Hellenic Sources* (Chapel Hill: University of North Carolina Press, 1971), 27.

8. Albert Camus, "Prometheus in the Underworld," in *Lyrical and Critical Essays,* 141.

9. Camus, *Notebooks 1942–1951,* trans. O'Brien, 136.

10. Albert Camus, *The Plague,* trans. Stuart Gilbert (New York: Vintage, 1991), 209.

11. Ibid., 39–40.

12. Ibid., 62.

13. Ibid., 247–248, 253–254.

14. Ibid., 180.

15. See, in particular, Archambault, *Camus' Hellenic Sources.* Yet Archambault concludes that Thucydides' presence in *The Plague* is limited to the Greek historian's methodology and his account of the plague.

16. Albert Camus, *Notebooks 1935–1942,* trans. Philip Thody (New York: Marlowe, 1998), 185.

17. Ibid., 193.

18. Quoted in Olivier Todd, *Albert Camus: Une vie* (Paris: Gallimard, 1996), 545.

19. Camus, *The Plague,* 236.

20. Ibid., 153.

21. Camus, *The Plague,* 138.

22. Thucydides, *History of the Peloponnesian War,* 159.

23. Ibid., 48.

24. W. Robert Connor, *Thucydides* (Princeton: Princeton University Press, 1984), 250.

25. Ibid., 247.

26. Camus, *The Plague,* 308.

27. Thucydides, *History of the Peloponnesian War,* 48.

28. Camus, *The Plague,* 308.

29. Ibid., 130.

30. Ibid., 127.

31. Ibid., 128.

32. Ibid., 131.

33. Thucydides, *History of the Peloponnesian War*, 402.

34. Ibid., 407.

35. Camus, *Notebooks 1942–1951*, trans. O'Brien, 56.

36. Jacqueline Lévi-Valensi, ed., *Camus at Combat: Writing 1944–1947*, trans. Arthur Goldhammer (Princeton: Princeton University Press, 2006), 287.

37. Thucydides, *History of the Peloponnesian War*, 147.

38. Camus, *The Plague*, 157.

39. Quoted in Ronald Aronson, *Camus and Sartre: The Story of a Friendship and the Quarrel That Ended It* (Chicago: University of Chicago Press, 2004), 54–55. I am deeply indebted in this chapter to Aronson's depiction of the friendship between the two writers.

40. Simone de Beauvoir, *A Transatlantic Love Affair*, quoted in Aronson, *Camus and Sartre*, 24.

41. See Aronson, *Camus and Sartre* (24), for a discussion of this event.

42. Todd, *Une vie*, 355. As Aronson rightly notes, Todd does not offer a source for this exchange.

43. Interview in *Les Nouvelles Littéraires*, November 15, 1945, in Camus, *Lyrical and Critical Essays*, 345.

44. Aronson, *Camus and Sartre*, 55.

45. Quoted in ibid., 37.

46. See Albert Camus, "La nausée de Jean-Paul Sartre," in *Essais*, ed. Roger Quilliot (Paris: Gallimard, 1965), 1417–1419.

47. Camus, *Notebooks 1942–1951*, trans. O'Brien, 24.

48. Camus, "Three Interviews," *Lyrical and Critical Essays*, 346.

49. Ibid., 346, 348.

50. Quoted in Rod Kedward, *France and the French* (New York: Overlook Press, 2005), 362.

51. Quoted in Tony Judt, *Postwar* (New York: Penguin, 2005), 197.

52. Simone de Beauvoir, *Force of Circumstance*, trans. Richard Howard (New York: Penguin, 1963), 243.

53. Quoted in Judt, *Postwar*, 221.

54. Beauvoir, *Force of Circumstance*, 265, 272.

55. Quoted in Todd, *Une vie*, 452.

56. Albert Camus, "The Deaf and Dumb Republic," in Lévi-Valensi, *Camus at Combat*, 280.

57. Albert Camus, "To Our Readers," in Lévi-Valensi, *Camus at Combat*, 292.

58. According to Aronson, Sartre treated "violence as a token of becoming real [and] focused on its positive political and psychological effects on those

who practice it, especially the victims of oppression, when all other paths became blocked." *Camus and Sartre,* 34.

59. Quoted in John Foley, *Albert Camus: From the Absurd to Revolt* (Montreal: McGill-Queen's University Press, 2008), 39.

60. Beauvoir, *Force of Circumstance,* 211.

61. Camus, *Notebooks 1942–1951,* trans. O'Brien, 147–148.

62. Ibid., 120–121.

63. Camus, *The Plague,* 128.

64. Ibid., 218.

65. Beauvoir, *Force of Circumstance,* 120.

66. Camus, *Notebooks 1942–1951,* trans. O'Brien, 211.

67. Albert Camus, *The Rebel,* trans. Anthony Bower (New York: Vintage, 1991), 4.

68. Ibid., 10.

69. Michel de Montaigne, *The Essays,* trans. Donald Frame (Palo Alto, CA: Stanford University Press, 1943), 323.

70. Montaigne, *The Essays,* 457.

71. Camus, *The Rebel,* 11.

72. Ibid., 236.

73. Foley, *From the Absurd to Revolt,* 32.

74. Camus, *The Rebel,* 22.

75. Ibid., 16.

76. Thucydides, *History of the Peloponnesian War,* 407.

77. Camus, *The Rebel,* 22.

78. Ibid., 27.

79. Ibid., 22.

80. Albert Camus, "Défense de *l'homme révolté,*" in *Essais,* 1705–1706.

81. Beauvoir, *Force of Circumstance,* 254.

82. Quoted in Judt, *Past Imperfect,* 117.

83. Beauvoir, *Force of Circumstance,* 273.

84. Quoted in Annie Cohen-Solal, *Sartre: A Life,* trans. Anna Cagnoni (New York: Pantheon, 1987), 328.

85. Letter to René Char (November 29, 1951), in Camus, *Essais,* 1627.

86. Quoted in Aronson, *Camus and Sartre,* 139.

87. Quoted in Todd, *Une vie,* 561.

88. Quoted in Foley, *From the Absurd to Revolt,* 112.

89. Aronson, *Camus and Sartre,* 142.

90. Albert Camus, "Révolte et servitude," letter to *Les Temps Modernes* (June 30, 1952), in *Essais,* 754.

91. Ibid., 758.

92. Ibid., 760–761.

93. Ibid., 771.

94. Ibid., 772.

95. Quoted in Lottman, *Albert Camus,* 531.

96. For a discussion of the Hume-Rousseau affair, see Robert Zaretsky and John T. Scott, *The Philosophers' Quarrel: Hume, Rousseau and the Limits of Human Understanding* (New Haven: Yale University Press, 2009).

97. Quoted in Lottman, *Albert Camus,* 531.

98. Quoted in Foley, *From the Absurd to Revolt,* 117.

99. Quoted in Ibid., 116.

100. Quoted in Aronson, *Camus and Sartre,* 38.

101. Lottman, *Albert Camus,* 532.

102. Quoted in Aronson, *Camus and Sartre,* 156.

103. Quoted in Todd, *Une vie,* 573.

104. Quoted in Ibid., 573–574. Aronson's translation mistakenly attributes the adjective *endormies* (numbing) to Camus's physical state rather than his thoughts. See Aronson, *Camus and Sartre,* 157.

105. Camus, *Notebooks 1951–1959,* trans. Ryan Bloom, 21, 26–28, 31, 47, 38.

106. Martha Nussbaum, *The Fragility of Goodness* (Cambridge, UK: Cambridge University Press, 1986), 35.

107. *The Oresteia,* trans. Robert Fagles (New York: Penguin, 1981), 267.

108. Nussbaum, *The Fragility of Goodness,* 49.

109. Camus, "Défense de *l'homme révolté,*" 1709–1710.

1956: Silence Follows

Epigraph. Albert Camus, "Review of Brice Parrain's *On a Philosophy of Expressions,*" in *Lyrical and Critical Essays,* trans. Philip Thody (New York: Knopf, 1968), 239.

1. Albert Camus, *Notebooks 1951–1959,* trans. Ryan Bloom (Chicago: Ivan Dee, 2008), 167.

2. Quoted in Alistair Horne, *A Savage War of Peace: Algeria, 1954–1962* (New York: Penguin, 1977), 27.

3. Jacqueline Lévi-Valensi identifies Camus's use of the term "inquiry" in both series of articles. See Jacqueline Lévi-Valensi, ed., *Camus at Combat: Writing 1944–1947,* trans. Arthur Goldhammer (Princeton: Princeton University Press, 2006), 199 n480.

4. Lévi-Valensi, *Camus at Combat,* 200, 205.

5. Ibid., 205.

6. Ibid., 205.

7. Ibid., 216.

8. Ibid., 209.

9. Ibid., 216.

10. *The Oresteia*, trans. Robert Fagles (New York: Penguin, 1981), 267.

11. Albert Camus, *The First Man*, trans. David Hapgood (New York: Knopf, 1995), 144–145.

12. Lévi-Valensi, *Camus at Combat*, 208.

13. Ibid., 215.

14. Albert Camus, "Réponse à Emmanuel d'Astier de la Vigerie," in *Essais*, ed. Roger Quilliot (Paris: Gallimard, 1965), 357.

15. Quoted in Horne, *Savage War of Peace*, 119.

16. Ibid., 120–122.

17. Albert Camus, *The Plague*, trans. Stuart Gilbert (New York: Vintage, 1991), 254.

18. Albert Camus, "Letter to an Algerian Militant," in *Resistance, Rebellion and Death*, trans. Justin O'Brien (New York: Knopf, 1963), 93–97.

19. "La table ronde," reprinted in *Essais*, 971.

20. Albert Camus, *Notebooks 1935–1942*, trans. Philip Thody (New York: Marlowe, 1998), 24 (May 1936). Here I am making use of Jeffrey Isaac's notion of "representative thinking." Isaac takes issue with Michael Walzer's claim that Camus valued—and rightly valued—*pied noir* lives more deeply than Muslim lives. See Jeffrey Isaac, *Arendt, Camus, and Modern Rebellion* (New Haven: Yale University Press, 1992), 194–206.

21. Albert Camus, "L'Algérie déchirée," in *Essais*, 985.

22. Quoted in Olivier Todd, *Albert Camus: Une vie* (Paris: Gallimard, 1996), 624–625n.

23. Albert Camus, introduction to *Actuelles I*, in *Essais*, 252.

24. Quoted in Jean Lacouture, *Pierre Mendès-France*, trans. George Holoch (New York: Holmes and Meier, 1984), 166.

25. Lacouture, *Pierre Mendès-France*, 334–335.

26. Quoted in Frank Giles, *The Locust Years* (London: Carroll & Graf, 1991), 273.

27. Jean Daniel, quoted in *Essais*, 1840.

28. Camus, *Notebooks 1951–1959*, trans. Ryan Bloom, 108.

29. "Appel pour une trêve civile en Algérie," in *Essais*, 991–999.

30. For the text of Camus's speech, see *Resistance, Rebellion and Death*, 97–106.

31. Herbert Lottman, *Albert Camus* (Corte Madera: Gingko Press, 1997), 604.

32. Quoted in Todd, *Une vie*, 630.

33. Camus, *Notebooks 1951–1959*, 175.

34. Albert Camus, *The Rebel*, trans. Anthony Bower (New York: Vintage, 1991), 166.

35. Ibid., 167.

36. Albert Camus, *The Just Assassins,* in *Caligula and Three Other Plays,* trans. Stuart Gilbert (New York: Vintage, 1958), 258.

37. Albert Camus, editorial in *L'Express* (October 21, 1954), in *Essais,* 973.

38. Todd, *Une vie,* 620.

39. Camus, *Notebooks 1951–1959,* 183.

40. Simone de Beauvoir, *Force of Circumstance,* trans. Richard Howard (New York: Penguin, 1963), 353–354.

41. Quoted in John Foley, *Albert Camus: From the Absurd to Revolt* (Montreal: McGill-Queen's University Press, 2008), 161.

42. Albert Camus, preface to *Germaine Tillion, Algeria: The Realities* (New York: Knopf, 1958), trans. Ronald Matthews, French version in Tzvetan Todorov, ed., *Le siècle de Germaine Tillion* (Paris: Seuil, 2007), 191. I have translated from the original French version.

43. See Jean Lacouture, "Au coeur de l'Algérie," in Todorov, *Le siècle de Germaine Tillion,* 197. Camus also provides a detailed account; see his *Notebooks 1951–1959,* 195–196.

44. Camus, *Notebooks 1951–1959,* 197.

45. Quoted in James Le Sueur, *Uncivil War: Intellectuals and Identity Politics during the Decolonization of Algeria* (Lincoln: University of Nebraska Press, 2001), 115–116.

46. Beauvoir, *Force of Circumstance,* 391–392, 396.

47. Camus, *Notebooks 1951–1959,* 68.

48. Letter to Jean Gillibert, quoted in Lottman, *Albert Camus,* 606.

49. Todd, *Une vie,* 685.

50. Camus, *Notebooks 1951–1959,* 96, emphasis in the original. In this case, Camus was defending Tunisians, not Algerians, but the lesson he took from the affair has general application.

51. Camus, *Notebooks 1951–1959,* 197. I have based my account on Lottman, *Albert Camus,* 631.

52. Camus, *Notebooks 1951–1959,* 197.

53. Quoted in Lottman, *Albert Camus,* 648.

54. Carl-Gustav Bjurstrom, postface to Albert Camus, *Discours de Suède* (Paris: Gallimard, 1997), 78.

55. *Le Monde,* December 14, 1957, in Camus, *Essais,* 1881–1882.

56. Quoted in Todd, *Une vie,* 701.

57. Beauvoir, *Force of Circumstance,* 396.

58. Camus, *Notebooks 1942–1951,* trans. O'Brien, 144.

59. Michael Walzer, *The Company of Critics* (New York: Basic Books, 1988), 146.

60. Jeffrey Isaac, I believe, is quite right to insist on this point: Camus sought to "occupy the no-man's land between the antagonists, the ground of a minimal common humanity that might support dialogue and mutual recognition" (195). John Foley offers a fuller and equally persuasive account of Isaac's position in his recent work. See his *From the Absurd to Revolt*, 160–166.

61. To the Algerian novelist Moulaud Feraoun, Camus confessed that between "wisdom reduced to silence and madness that shouts itself hoarse, I prefer the virtues of silence." Quoted in Lottman, *Albert Camus*, 657.

62. *Confessions*, book I, chap. 4, trans. Rex Warner (New York: Penguin, 1963), 19.

63. In *Une vie*, Todd notes repeatedly Camus's ignorance of Wittgenstein's work (e.g., 293). At the same time, there is no trace of recognition of Camus's work in Wittgenstein.

64. Ray Monk, *Ludwig Wittgenstein: The Duty of Genius* (New York: Free Press, 1990), 282.

65. Monk, *Ludwig Wittgenstein*, 156.

66. Quoted in Monk, *Ludwig Wittgenstein*, 277.

67. Albert Camus, "Return to Tipasa," in *Lyrical and Critical Essays*, 169–170.

68. Tony Judt, *The Burden of Responsibility* (Chicago: University of Chicago Press, 1998), 120.

69. *Le Monde*, December 17, 1957, in Camus, *Essais*, 1883.

70. Walzer, *The Company of Critics*, 152.

71. Camus, *Discours de Suède*, 26.

72. Quoted in Paul Archambault, *Camus' Hellenic Sources* (Chapel Hill: University of North Carolina Press, 1971), 32.

Epilogue

Epigraph. Albert Camus, *Notebooks: 1935–1942*, trans. Philip Thody (New York: Marlowe, 1998), 119–120.

1. "The Guest," in *Exile and the Kingdom*, trans. Carol Cosman (New York: Vintage, 2006), 75.

2. Ibid., 76

3. Ibid., 76–77.

4. Ibid., 78.

5. Ibid., 78.

6. Ibid., 79.

7. Ibid., 84–85.

8. Ibid., 85.

9. Ibid., 86.

10. Ibid., 73.

11. Ibid., 75–75.

12. Ibid., 74.

13. Ibid., 77.

14. Iris Murdoch, *The Sovereignty of Good* (London: Routledge, 1970), 23.

15. Ibid., 34.

16. Albert Camus, *Notebooks 1951–1959*, trans. Ryan Bloom (Chicago: Ivan Dee, 2008), 186.

17. Simone Weil, "Gravity and Grace," in Siân Miles, ed., *Simone Weil: An Anthology* (New York: Weidenfeld & Nicolson, 1986), 216.

18. Albert Camus, "Between Yes and No," in *Lyrical and Critical Essays*, trans. Ellen Kennedy (New York: Knopf, 1968), 78.

19. Jeffrey Isaac, *Arendt, Camus and Modern Rebellion* (New Haven: Yale University Press, 1992), 118.

20. Albert Camus, introduction to *Actuelles I*, in *Oeuvres complètes*, vol. I: *Essais*, ed. Roger Quilliot (Paris: Gallimard, 1965), 252.

INDEX